Leading with Character and Competence

Leading with Character and Competence

Moving Beyond Title, Position, and Authority

Timothy R. Clark

Berrett–Koehler Publishers, Inc.
a BK Business book

Berrett-Koehler Publishers, Inc.
1333 Broadway, Suite 1000, Oakland, CA 94612-1921
Tel: (510) 817-2277   Fax: (510) 817-2278   www.bkconnection.com

Ordering Information

Quantity sales. Special discounts are available on quantity purchases by corporations, associations, and others. For details, contact the "Special Sales Department" at the Berrett-Koehler address above.

Individual sales. Berrett-Koehler publications are available through most bookstores. They can also be ordered directly from Berrett-Koehler:

Tel: (800) 929-2929; Fax: (802) 864-7626; www.bkconnection.com.

Orders for college textbook/course adoption use. Please contact Berrett-Koehler:

Tel: (800) 929-2929; Fax: (802) 864-7626.

Orders by U.S. trade bookstores and wholesalers. Please contact Ingram Publisher Services, Tel: (800) 509-4887; Fax: (800) 838-1149; E-mail: customer.service@ingrampublisherservices.com; or visit www.ingram publisherservices.com/Ordering for details about electronic ordering.

Berrett-Koehler and the BK logo are registered trademarks of Berrett-Koehler Publishers, Inc.

Printed in the United States of America

Berrett-Koehler books are printed on long-lasting acid-free paper. When it is available, we choose paper that has been manufactured by environmentally responsible processes. These may include using trees grown in sustainable forests, incorporating recycled paper, minimizing chlorine in bleaching, or recycling the energy produced at the paper mill.

Library of Congress Cataloging-in-Publication Data
Names: Clark, Timothy R., 1964– author.
Title: Leading with character and competence : moving beyond title, position, and authority / Timothy R. Clark.
Description: First Edition. | Oakland : Berrett-Koehler Publishers, 2016. | Includes bibliographical references and index.
Identifiers: LCCN 2016022358 | ISBN 9781626567733 (hardcover)
Subjects: LCSH: Leadership.
Classification: LCC HD57.7 .C5377 2016 | DDC 658.4/092—dc23
LC record available at https://lccn.loc.gov/2016022358

20   19   18   17   16   10   9   8   7   6   5   4   3   2   1

Cover design by Karen Marquardt. Interior design and composition by Gary Palmatier, Ideas to Images. Elizabeth von Radics, copyeditor; Mike Mollett, proofreader; Rachel Rice, indexer.

To Tracey

Contents

Preface

WHEN YOU LOOK IN THE MIRROR, DO YOU SEE A LEADER? Can you see the unfolded vision of what you can become? I am convinced that most people do not comprehend their leadership potential. I wrote this book to help you realize that potential. For that to happen, you will need to unmask the false concept that leadership is about title, position, and authority. These are worldly artifacts. They have their place, but the journey of becoming a better leader is not about those things. It's about elevating your thoughts, beliefs, and actions to a higher plane. It's about deep introspection and self-discovery born of a desire to make a difference in the world. Regrettably, the moral fog and materialism of our day try to convince us to measure leadership by the wrong standards. There must be a confrontation with these counterfeit claims.

Regardless of who you are, you must build your foundation on two things: character and competence. This is a universal truth. Leadership is about following principles. You either follow the principles or break yourself against them. The principles themselves don't break. Nor do they negotiate.

Great leaders are built from the inside. You must start with *character.* The four cornerstones of character are *integrity, humility, accountability,* and *courage.* Then comes *competence.* The four cornerstones of competence are *learning, change, judgment,* and *vision.*

Leadership is not an easy education. How could it be? It is the most important applied discipline in the world. It has its price: consistent, rigorous, and deliberate effort. In fact, it mocks our attempts to get it cheap. You will have to unlearn and abandon some of your current thinking and behavior. At times you will stumble in your pursuit, and your weaknesses will be exposed. But if you are determined, you will accelerate your progress. You will lead with the intent to contribute rather than consume, bless rather than impress. You will literally change people's lives and leave a legacy that lingers far into the future.

This is the epic story of leadership.

Leading with Character and Competence Self-Assessment

To jump-start your leadership journey, I suggest taking the companion self-assessment after reading this book. The self-assessment will give you a baseline measure of your own character and competence and help you identify development priorities for creating a personal action plan. Please see the Leading with Character and Competence Self-Assessment on page 187.

Introduction

Titles are shadows, crowns are empty things.

Daniel Defoe (1660–1731)
English trader, writer, journalist, and spy
The True-Born Englishman (1701)

LEADERSHIP IS A TOPIC CROWDED WITH ABSURD THEORIES. Over the years we have celebrated the absurdities. We have jumped from one superstition to another. We've bedeviled ourselves with trends and fashions. We've changed "hues and views to fit the situation."[1] Out of a simple concept, we have created a myth-making industry, a platitudinous art, an intellectual toy. We've made it too complicated, and in many cases the theories we've hatched are dangerously misleading. Consider the following strains of thought.

Ten Misleading Leadership Theories

1. **Leadership is about charisma.** If you have personal magnetism, dash, and style, you are a leader.

2. **Leadership is about eloquence.** If you have Churchillian powers of expression, you are a leader.

3. **Leadership is about power.** If you are a chief executive officer (CEO) or a bemedaled general, you are a leader.

4. **Leadership is about seniority.** If you have outlived everyone else, you are a leader.

5. **Leadership is about scale.** If you work on the important issues of the day, you are a leader.

6. **Leadership is about popularity.** If everyone likes you, you are a leader.

7. **Leadership is about fame.** If you are known far and wide, you are a leader.

8. **Leadership is about winning.** If you have beat your opponents, you are a leader.

9. **Leadership is about wealth.** If you have money, you are a leader.

10. **Leadership is about education.** If you are degreed and credentialed, you are a leader.

I know people who possess all of these things and are not leaders. I know others who possess none of these things and are. These ideas represent bad philosophy, and, as writer C. S. Lewis said, "bad philosophy needs to be answered."[2]

It needs to be answered because otherwise people go away confused and discouraged. I'm not saying these things have nothing to do with leadership. They may point at the possibility, but they make no promises. Frankly, we have yet to recover from these seductive delusions.

The Essence of Leadership

What, then, is the kernel of this concept we call leadership? Novelist and Nobel laureate Thomas Mann wrote, "Order and simplification are the first steps toward the mastery of a subject."[3]

I have asked thousands of people around the world this simple question: *What single word best captures the concept of leadership?* Put on some noise-cancelling headphones while I tell you the answer. Leadership is not an ethereal concept. It is not as cinematic as you might think. It's about one simple and profoundly human thing: *influence.*

Yes, the essence of leadership is influence.

But it's not just any kind of influence. It must aim at something good, something noble, something that builds, lifts, and makes better. In its purest sense, leadership is about influencing people to climb, stretch, and become. And it's not about the scope of your stewardship; influencing the one is just as worthy as influencing the many.

For example, I crashed into another car driving out of a parking lot the other day. It was my fault. What happened next was stunning. The man whose car I hit was perfectly calm and unstintingly kind. I smashed his Lexus and ruined his day, and here he was, setting an example of patience and composure. It was a simple, brief, one-on-one encounter and yet an awesome display of influence and a clinic in leadership.

How do you exercise leadership? How do you generate this kind of influence? Not much to demystify here. The mechanism is primarily modeling behavior. It's about walking the talk through your living, breathing example. Psychologist Albert Bandura captured the principle: "Most human behavior is learned observationally through modeling: from observing others, one forms an idea of how new behaviors are performed, and on later occasions this coded information serves as a guide for action."[4]

Humans are social animals. We influence one another in a continuous, uninterruptible, and reciprocal process. You cannot wake up and say, "I don't want to influence anyone today." If you are interacting with people, you are influencing them and they are influencing you. Even your absence influences others.

The question is: *How will you influence and toward what end will you influence?* This fact never changes, but the conditions around us do. Increasingly, we influence under conditions of radical transparency. Andrew Liveris, CEO of Dow Chemical,

Figure I.1 The Spectrum of Influence

| Manipulation | Persuasion | Coercion |

observes, "Now, the judge, the jury, the trial, the media, the speed of life, the world of social media—everything you do is scrutinized. Every word you utter, every place you go, what you do, how you do it."[5]

Think about influence on a spectrum (see figure I.1). At one end is *manipulation.* To influence through manipulation is to use deception to gain advantage. Manipulation can be mild and well meaning, as when a mother alternates apple sauce and pureed carrots on the spoon when feeding her baby. It can also be predatory and destructive, as when payday loan companies lure the working poor into misleading contracts that charge usurious interest rates and trap them in a cycle of debt.

At the other end of the spectrum is *coercion.* People who coerce others press them into service. They muscle and force their way to achieve their aims. I once had a football coach at this end of the spectrum. Ironically, he would scream and demean and use abuse as his primary means of calling forth peak performance in his players.

Whereas manipulation exploits through subtle means, coercion controls through brute force. Here's the principle: if you try to influence people through manipulation or coercion, you have abandoned legitimate forms of influence. You are not leading anymore.

In the middle of the spectrum is *persuasion*—the realm of true leadership.

If you lay down your tricks (manipulation) and your power tools (coercion), what else is there? The answer is persuasion based on character and competence. Out of character flows the confidence that you can be trusted to do the job. Out of competence flows the confidence that you know how to do the job. A great leader influences through the combined credibility of character and competence—no duplicity, no intimidation, no fear, no threats, and no betrayal.

Thirty years ago I served as a missionary in Korea. My first assignment was to go to the rural province of Kang Won and apprentice with an experienced native Korean missionary named Soe Yang Shik. It was a humorous case of the West and the East coming together. I was 6 foot 5 inches tall. He was 5 foot 5 inches tall. I couldn't speak Korean. He couldn't speak English. And then it all began. We worked from sunup till sundown. He helped me learn the language. He helped me learn to use my chopsticks so I wouldn't starve. He taught me how to plan, organize, and carry out humanitarian projects. He taught me how to teach and serve people. To this day he stands as one of my greatest mentors. How did he do it? He did it without manipulation or coercion. It was pure and powerful persuasion based on a combination of character and competence.

People perceive influence patterns in others very quickly. If you get a new boss, coach, teacher, or friend, you observe that individual. You look for influence patterns and then apply predictive analytics based on what you see. Intuitively, you run a trust equation and respond accordingly. If you see patterns of manipulation or coercion, you naturally retreat and focus on risk management, self-preservation, and pain avoidance. If, on the other hand, that person promotes psychological safety through patterns of persuasion, you respond with trust, commitment, and higher performance. You reciprocate with more discretionary effort. You do not trust power; you rely on the power of trust.

Leadership Is an Applied Discipline

Now consider the oppressive myth that leadership is about title, position, and authority. These things are merely accessories. In this world we elect presidents, appoint CEOs, and, in about four dozen cases, still crown kings and queens. But there is no coronation of leaders in the true sense of the word. To robe yourself in the outward vestments of a leader does not make you one. That kind of equipment is visible evidence of power, but please do not mistake it for leadership. The formal conferral of authority no more makes you a leader than a black turtleneck makes you the CEO of a tech company. Rank can only hint at the possibility. That's all.

I meet scores of individual contributors who are convinced that they are not leaders because they possess no formal status. I also meet scores of managers who think they *are* simply because they do. Both groups are terribly wrong.

Under intensifying pressure to become flat, lean, and competitive, organizations today ask employees at every level to step up and be leaders—to lead from every level, every seat, and every role. And yet most employees hold no title, position, or authority. It doesn't matter. Leaders who develop character and competence become scalable in their impact, regardless of their role. In business organizations, governments, schools, and families, they become force multipliers. They create more value for their organizations, more success for others, and more opportunities for themselves.

Leadership is an applied discipline, not a foamy concept. In fact, it is the single most important applied discipline in the world. It's a factor in every decision and every outcome. In every human collective—the family, the fourth-grade classroom, the multinational corporation, the repertory dance theatre, the start-up, and the monkish order—performance is always traceable to leadership. And true leadership is always traceable to influence based on credibility forged from character and competence.

Leadership is the most engaging, inspiring, and deeply satisfying activity known to humankind. Through leadership we have the opportunity to progress, overcome adversity, change lives, and bless the species. The beautiful thing about leadership is that anyone can aspire to it. It's within reach if you are willing to learn, work, and get out of your own way. Leadership scholars Warren Bennis and Burt Nanus wrote, "The truth is that major capacities and competencies of leadership can be learned.... Whatever natural endowments we bring to the role of leadership, they *can* be enhanced."[6]

Character and Competence

To become a better leader, you will need both character and competence—character to influence positively and competence to influence effectively. The two bleed into each other. Having one does not cancel the need for the other or compensate for a lack of the other. Leaders do not make decisions based on character or competence alone. The two domains are overlapping magisteria: the heart and the head, motive and skill, intent and technique, moral strength and intellectual horsepower.

For example, *judgment* is a combination of integrity and knowledge. *Productivity* is a combination of discipline and skill. *Collaboration* is a combination of humility and communication. Character needs competence and competence needs character. Character is the core. Competence is the crust. Together they represent leadership's irreducible minimum (see figure I.2).

Character represents the truth of who you are and what you stand for. It's a basic measure of your moral makeup and the degree to which you govern yourself from the inside based on

Figure I.2 The Core of Character and the Crust of Competence

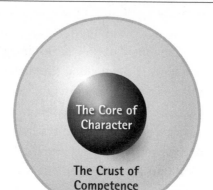

values and a self-imposed ethical creed. William Wordsworth described the leader of character as one

> Whose high endeavors are an inward light
> That makes the path before him always bright.[7]

The core of character does not have anything to do with technical expertise, charismatic arts, grasp of strategy, or a host of other technical and professional stuff. That kind of skill, knowledge, experience—that's all competence. Abraham Lincoln is purported to have said, "Character is like a tree and reputation like its shadow. The shadow is what we think of it, but the tree is the real thing."

When we speak of character, we are talking about the unvarnished, unedited truth of how you think and behave, as well as how you regard and treat yourself and other people. It flows from the empire of the heart.

Think about high-profile leaders. Name a spectacular fall from grace that was about a lack of competence. When leaders go down hard, they go down from the inside out. It's a collapse of character, a core meltdown. Would you rather go into battle with a charismatic leader with a liquid core or a dull leader with a titanium center? British statesman Thomas Macaulay once said of himself, "It is not necessary to my happiness that I should sit in Parliament; but it is necessary to my happiness that I should possess, in Parliament or out of Parliament, the consciousness of having done what is right."[8]

That is a man of character speaking.

It is more than antiquarian charm to say that leaders should be honest and morally excellent. Society depends on it. That is why leadership *is* the ultimate applied discipline, and being a good one is the worthy quest of a lifetime. There is no shortcut, formula, or tonic. Becoming a great leader requires honest toil— social, emotional, intellectual, and moral exertion. The process is simple but not easy. Don't confuse the two.

The Four Types of Leaders

A character-plus-competence conception of leadership produces four types of leaders that have nothing to do with title, position, or authority. Rather these types describe how a leader feels, thinks, and behaves. If you look around, you will see that leaders do indeed cluster around these four types (see figure I.3).

Great leaders (high character + high competence). If you are strong on both accounts, you have the opportunity to make a difference—a positive and substantial difference in the lives of those around you—through your influence. This should be your goal. Strong character and competence will bring greater depth and breadth to your offering as a leader. It will allow you to make your fullest and finest contribution.

Specifically, a strong core will keep you safe from your own betrayal. It will allow you to avoid excessive affectation, jealous ambition, and a love affair with power. To have strong character

Figure I.3 The Four Types of Leaders

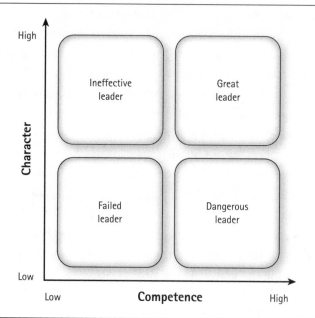

and competence is to have both the intent and the capacity to make an impact. The lack of leaders in this category is society's most acute need.

Ineffective leaders (high character + low competence). An ineffective leader is a person of basic upright character who unfortunately lacks the skills. The typical pattern of an ineffective leader is a lack of drive rather than a lack of intellect. Leaders in this category have a morbid propensity to procrastinate. Out of fear, entitlement, or laziness, ineffective leaders avoid exertion. They consistently refuse to leave their comfort zones and stretch to their outer limits. Ineffective leaders who have drive do not remain ineffective for long. They get better, even if at a slow pace.

Nobel Prize–winning economist Daniel Kahneman asserts, "Laziness is built deep into our nature."[9] I would qualify that and say that laziness is built into our physical and mental makeup, but those who are determined can overcome it and develop astonishing discipline. Even the least gifted leaders can escape incompetence with raw effort. Unfortunately, the number of ineffective leaders is growing as the pace of change accelerates. You can find yourself in the ineffective category by simply standing still. Just coast awhile, and your relevance will melt away as you slip into a cycle of obsolescence.

We may trust incompetent leaders personally, but we can't trust them professionally. They may be our friends, and we may have great affection for them, but we can't rely on them to lead us, particularly in the accelerated, compressed, and volatile twenty-first century. We don't have that kind of margin for error. The risk is too great and the stakes are too high.

Failed leaders (low character + low competence). Failed leaders misspend their lives primarily because they refuse to hold themselves accountable. Rather than reflect on their performance in the spirit of humility and openness, they ignore feedback and deflect personal responsibility. This is the root of their failure: They never learn to delay gratification, acknowledge the inherent value of other people, or respect the principles of work and earned achievement. They hold but one conviction—a sense of their own entitlement. You will often find that they have risen to positon through flattery and the trading of favors.

Failed leaders crave rank because they can hide behind it and wage a war of self-preservation. Devoid of purpose outside of themselves, failed leaders are imposters who feed on aggrandizement. They advocate privilege based on position and connections because they cannot claim leadership on merit and they have no desire to. They are counterfeits, imposters, and pharisees devoted to image and appearance.

Dangerous leaders (low character + high competence). It's one thing to have immoral intent, but what happens when you combine corruption with skill? A dangerous leader is a person who splices intelligence with crooked character—a clever person with undiminished ambition and unrestrained moral ties, a person who trades integrity for money, economic man personified, a creature who obsesses on maximizing personal gain, a human vending machine.

I hear people say that leaders need to be authentic and true to what they believe in. What if you don't believe in anything but yourself?[10] By definition, your leadership will be manipulative or coercive. Out of a mercenary spirit, you will seek to use people rather than serve them, as many malevolent geniuses have done in what becomes a struggle for power or, as one author calls it, "the battle of cold steel."[11]

I had a famous professor at Oxford make this terrifying statement: "My colleagues and I agree on almost nothing, but the one thing we do agree on is not to believe in anything too much." Leaders who do not believe in anything are susceptible to becoming profoundly self-absorbed and dedicating their lives to the unquenchable pursuit of self-interest. As dangerous leaders mischannel their drive, they become a growing menace to their fellows. Some become human jackals. Many of the most commanding leaders in history—those who have wielded vast influence over humankind, and many with appalling capacity—have been members of this type. They become petty tyrants who mouth big ideas, drawing people under their spell from the dark side of charisma.

When a leader has significant capacity and directs that capacity toward dark, selfish, or trivial ends, people and performance suffer. Teddy Roosevelt captured the essence of the dangerous leader when he said, "Courage, intellect, all the masterful qualities, serve but to make a man more evil if they are merely used for that man's own advancement."[12]

In our day business magnate and philanthropist Warren Buffett put it this way: "In looking for people to hire, you look for three qualities: integrity, intelligence, and energy. And if they don't have the first, the other two will kill you."[13] Talented people especially seem to have a highly developed sense of smell for dangerous leaders; if a leader doesn't pass the character smell test, they resist that leader's influence or simply leave.

Becoming a Great Leader

What activist and philosopher Thomas Paine said of freedom applies equally to leadership: "What we obtain too cheap, we esteem too lightly: it is dearness only that gives everything its value. Heaven knows how to put a proper price upon its goods."[14] Neither character nor competence is free. The good news is that leadership does not require the credentials of title, position, or authority. Nor are you birthmarked a leader. Leadership is a learnable skill. It comes down to your patterns of belief, thought, and behavior and how those patterns influence others.

In this book we consider both character and competence. In part one we discuss the four cornerstones of character: integrity, humility, accountability, and courage. In part two we talk about the four cornerstones of competence: learning, change, judgment, and vision. Are there other attributes of character and competence? Of course. My purpose here is to address the threshold requirements. Your part is to take personal inventory and make sustainable behavioral change on the path of becoming a better leader.

Making Sustainable Behavioral Change

I offer the following three suggestions for making sustainable behavioral change.

Own your own development. First keep in mind the iron law of personal development: *All sustainable personal development is based on a transfer of ownership to the individual.* This means that nothing happens until you find a deep personal commitment to make it happen. If you own it, you can achieve positive behavioral change and sustain it. If you don't, the shelf life of emotion will expire and you'll experience the classic failure pattern that we call a *regression to the mean.* You will simply revert to your old equilibrium and comfort zone.

Maintain no more than two or three development priorities at a time. A portion of my personal consulting practice involves coaching executives. From my accumulated experience, it's clear that a person can only focus on only two or three things at a time. I have seen individuals get a little too excited and come back to me with five or six development goals. That kind of scope is developmentally overwhelming, dangerously dilutes effort, and leads to discouragement and failure. Make your goals specific and behavioral, create detailed plans to improve, and give them intense focus and disproportionate attention.

Keep a clean mirror. Begin your personal development process with a healthy dose of *self-awareness*—an enabling precondition for personal development. Without it you have no bearings to comprehend your true position, so there's a good chance you will wander without solid and cumulative progress over time. But if you carefully examine yourself and maintain a diet of undiluted feedback, you will move the needle.

How to Read this Book

I am not offering a step-by-step, turnkey solution because the quest to become a better leader is not a tidy, linear process. You can't package leadership like a diet or an exercise regimen. Improvement is a gritty, lifelong process, and we are all in different stages, working on different things. You have my permission to start reading anywhere. If you need to work on humility, read that chapter first. If developing better judgment is your priority, go there. I hope you'll see the book as an on-demand resource that you can read based on need.

PART ONE

The Four Cornerstones of Character

LEADERSHIP BEGINS WITH CHARACTER. IF YOU START building competence without the footings and foundation of character in place, you will implode when there's pressure, stress, or the temptation to accept an unearned reward.

Integrity

The first cornerstone of character is integrity. *Integrity* is about basic honesty and squaring up to who you are and what you believe. Integrity accelerates your personal development as you avoid feigned attempts to be amoral. When you avoid ethical misconduct and self-justification, your modeling behavior becomes astonishingly powerful. You deal justly with others because you deal justly with yourself. You put forth your best personal effort. You are careful to take credit and generous in giving it.

Humility

The second cornerstone of character is humility. *Humility* is a companion to integrity and is the unresented acknowledgment of your own dependency and ignorance. It's the capacity to avoid hubris and the reality distortion field it creates. The more humility you have, the clearer your thoughts and the cleaner your actions. Humility does three amazing things: First, it keeps you safe from the perils of your own ego. Second, it brings you more satisfaction as you rejoice in the success of others. Third, it makes you more willing and able to change.

Accountability

The third cornerstone of character is accountability. Great leaders are not only willing but eager to be answerable for their results. Isn't it interesting that poor leaders hate to be measured and great leaders can't wait? When you model the principle of *accountability*, you do not deflect personal responsibility, you understand that hiding is a false concept, and you always assume that private choices leak into public consequences. Finally, accountability means finishing what you start and resisting all forms of entitlement along the way.

Courage

The fourth and final cornerstone of character is courage. To have *courage* is to resist and challenge the forces of the status quo when necessary. You are the one who has to upend the state of affairs and rebel against the popular culture. You are the creator, not the caretaker. You have a heavier social, emotional, intellectual, spiritual, and physical burden to bear. You avoid the *soft quit*—where you deliberately lessen your effort and eliminate any chance of success—and maintain the discipline to make something happen. Finally, you have the courage to set *stretch goals* that fire the imagination.

CHAPTER 1

The First Cornerstone
of Character:

Integrity

*I prefer to be true to myself, even at the hazard
of incurring the ridicule of others, rather than to
be false, and incur my own abhorrence.*

Frederick Douglass (1818–1895)
African-American social reformer, abolitionist, orator, writer, and statesman
The Narrative of the Life of Frederick Douglass (1845)

Our Integrity Problem

The first cornerstone of character is integrity—but let's not get philosophical about what that means. We are talking about basic, straight-up honesty. Unfortunately, corruption is the pandemic of our time.[1] Most nations on planet Earth are deeply and almost irretrievably corrupt. They have become undrainable swamps. Greek philosopher Aristotle said, "The mass of citizens is less corruptible than the few."[2] For the sake of civil society, we need that to be true. Yet according to the Edelman Trust Barometer, three out of four institutions globally are losing the public's trust.[3]

Consider that in this country we are chasing after dreamy egalitarianism with fiscal recklessness. We like rights and dislike responsibility. With our no-fault philosophy, we suffer from the tyranny of tolerance. We have adopted a spray-on-tan culture of YOLO narcissism. Indeed, if we can clear the decks of right and wrong—disavow, repudiate, and savage the concepts—we can give ourselves permission to do anything we want.[4] And if we want to sound erudite about it, we call morality "cultural relativism."[5] As one observer said, "As truth has been relativized—absolutely relativized, so to speak—so has morality."[6]

We have a hard time being honest about the problem. We would rather extend our adolescent play of the mind. The truth is that our compass-free society is immoral in its feigned attempts to be amoral. As political thinker and historian Alexis de Tocqueville said of the Old World, we can say of the new: We are "untroubled by those muddled and incoherent concepts of good and evil."[7]

The Broken Triangle

We all come with a preinstalled moral sense, yet we still need to be taught integrity because it requires skill and vigilance to maintain it. We learn integrity by seeing it in action. Our children have to learn it the same way. Regrettably, as a society we are not teaching and modeling integrity to the next generation as we should. Religiosity has waned, and most schools are mandated by law to play neutral. If we yield to this "wintry piece of fact,"[8] we have to admit that the three institutions of home, church, and school—these agents that represented the triangle of socialization and have for centuries carried the burden of imbuing the next generation with integrity—are broken. This largely explains our demoralization, which is a predictable consequence of our willingness to embrace the delusion of amorality, or permissiveness thinly disguised.[9]

With the triangle of socialization broken, we have, as political scientist James Q. Wilson asserts, amputated our public discourse on morality at the knees.[10] And the predatory media is happy to step in as a surrogate to teach secular humanism and its popular corruptions—namely, the norms of gain and glory, indulgence, self-aggrandizement, and a hundred forms of venality. Not surprisingly, many of society's young think that integrity is unrealistic and perhaps even quaint. They may discount it as Disney idealism because they have been taught that a serious person plays to win.[11] Indeed, ours has become a cowardly culture in which everyone forbids everyone to make value judgments.[12]

You Will Be Tested

On one occasion I was training leaders at a Fortune 500 corporation. I brought a large FOR SALE sign into the room, the kind you would plant in your front yard. I gave it to one of the leaders and asked, "Are *you* for sale?" Then I paused and said, "If you don't have an ethical creed that goes to your marrow and says, 'some things are not for sale at any price,' you are for sale. You will go to the highest bidder."

Through the course of your personal and professional life, you will run an ethical gauntlet. Your integrity will be tested. You will be propositioned to lie, steal, cheat, extort, bribe, indulge, silence, swindle, defraud, scam, evade, and exploit. Even if you don't go looking, the opportunities for ethical misconduct will find you. At the very least, you will be asked to remain purse-lipped and silent as you witness soft forms of crooked behavior around you.

Anticipate the obstacles. Prepare for their arrival. When an ethical dilemma presents itself in the moment, the situation suddenly becomes pressurized. Negotiators call it "deal heat." Be ready for that dialed-up intensity. And be alert because ethical issues do not announce themselves. Howard Winkler, manager of ethics and compliance at Southern Company, said, "When an ethical issue arises, it does not come gift-wrapped with a note that says, 'This is an ethical issue. Prepare to make an ethical decision.' It just comes across as another business problem that needs to be solved."[13]

Know too that at least once in your life you will face a monumental obstacle, a severe trial, a crucible affliction that will try your integrity to the breaking point. You may well experience, as writer Victor Hugo said of his character Jean Valjean in *Les Miserables,* "the pressure of disproportionate misfortune."[14] That day comes for all of us when our integrity goes on trial. It came for Sir Walter Scott, the beloved Scottish writer, when his publishing house failed and he found himself buried under crushing debt. In his personal journal, he described it this way: "Yet God knows, I am at sea in the dark, and the vessel leaky."[15]

Do You Have a Personal Magna Carta?

Albert Schweitzer, the great humanitarian and Nobel Peace Prize winner, studied ethics and said the experience "left me dangling in midair."[16] *Ethics,* which is a branch of philosophy, likes to ruminate about what is right and wrong, but it steadfastly refuses to tell you what to do. Don't worry, you can't read your way to integrity, anyway.

Yes, we face some very complex ethical issues in our day. But most of the time, acting with integrity is not about knowing what to do; it's simply about doing it. The ability to perform moral reasoning does not make you moral; it's *doing* what is moral that makes you moral. For example, in a recent survey in the United Kingdom, students were asked, "Would you cheat in an exam if you knew you wouldn't get caught?" Fifty-nine percent of those surveyed said, "Yeah, sure," while only 41 percent said, "No way."[17] Do these students lack moral-reasoning skills?

As a human being, you confront moral choices that test your integrity. Leaders with integrity govern themselves. They regulate their own behavior and impose their own limits. They do not lie, steal, or cheat because they know it's inherently wrong. They have a *personal* Magna Carta to stand on principle.[18] People flock to their high standards and taproot convictions.

But if you are unsworn to principles, integrity vanishes. As professor Harvey Mansfield wrote, "When choice is without any principle to guide it, those who must make a choice look around for something to replace principle."[19] That search will often come back to the pursuit of selfish interest. If you don't stand for principle, there is simply nothing left to stand on. You will accept the unprincipled gain and reject the principled loss.

Leaders without integrity must be regulated from the outside by rules, laws, compliance systems, organs of restraint, and the larger control environment around them. They also know innately that lying, stealing, and cheating are wrong. They know the principle but refuse to be governed by it. Surely you have seen how people behave in riots. As the risk/reward ratio shifts, as the deterrence and the threat of punishment disappear, people burn cars and loot the neighborhood store. There's no internal check on behavior. It's a base and primal response.

The Four Moral Navigators diagram shows how people make moral decisions, using four devices that have an impact on their behavior (see figure 1.1).

- **Consequences (gain or pain).** With this navigator we attempt to think through a course of action and its consequences. We forecast the pain or gain associated with a given choice. If the reward is high and the risk is low, we move toward the reward.

- **Rules and laws.** With this navigator we look for rules and laws that apply to a given course of action and allow ourselves to be governed by them.

- **Peer influence and social norms.** With this navigator we are guided by the influence of those around us. We sense and follow the norms, mores, and expectations of society or the organization to which we belong.

Figure 1.1 The Four Moral Navigators

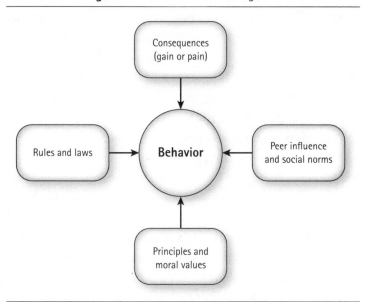

- **Principles and moral values.** With this navigator we consult and follow principles and moral values implanted in our hearts and minds. We act out of a conviction of what is right or wrong, regardless of outside pressure, influence, or temptation.

Each device is important and has a role to play, but to maintain integrity, principles and moral values must have the last word. The person or organization without integrity suspends principles and moral values while applying the other navigational devices. For example, why did Volkswagen executives decide to manipulate their diesel engine software to control emissions only during laboratory testing but not in real-world driving? They applied the first device—consequences—and suspended the other three. They were lured by the prospect of financial gain.

Integrity must be rooted in your understanding of leadership: Leaders with integrity lead to contribute. Leaders without integrity lead to consume. There will be times, at least in the short term, when integrity is expensive, when it costs you something. It's hard to bravely refuse what we know is wrong when it rewards us. And it's hard to do what we know is right when it costs us. Author and columnist Peggy Noonan was correct when she said, "You can't rent a strong moral sense."[20] Actually, you can't even buy one. You have to develop it. You have to work at it, model it, teach it, and defend it. It takes integrity to withstand the seductions of our day.

Daniel Vasella, the CEO of Swiss pharmaceutical giant Novartis, addresses integrity directly and explicitly with his people: "I talk to my team about the seductions that come with taking on a leadership role. There are many different forms: sexual seduction, money, praise. You need to be aware of how you can be seduced in order to be able to resist and keep your integrity."[21]

Rocks and Trees Are Neutral

Theologian John Calvin wrote in 1536, "The minds of all men have impressions of civil order and honesty."[22] And yet we are dual beings. We have impulses to do good and impulses to do evil—and we know the difference. The problem is we don't always act on what we know. The great Russian novelist Alexander Solzhenitsyn said that we have created "an atmosphere of moral mediocrity, paralyzing man's noblest impulses."[23]

Integrity is a matter of will.[24] You have to want it more than you want whatever else is on offer. Journalist and politician Horace Greeley said, "Fame is a vapor; popularity an accident; riches take wings."[25] Do you believe that? This is not a philosophical question. You will have to answer that question today. You cannot stand on the sidelines and pretend to be above the fray.

Maybe your parents didn't inculcate in you the importance of values. Maybe you've had role models who taught you to subcontract your moral reflections.[26] Maybe you had a boss whose only permanent loyalty was to himself. Maybe the mass media taught you to gorge on power and profits. Maybe greed has dulled your senses. Maybe you had a philosophy professor who taught you there are no fixed principles.[27] Maybe you know people who cheat and prosper.[28] Maybe you're disoriented by the morally malignant air you breathe. Maybe you hold your nose as you look at a rogues' gallery of retrograde characters and "the long freak show that was 20th-century world leadership."[29]

Maybe. But you cannot be neutral. Rocks and trees are neutral—not people. You can't wash your hands and be a philosopher. As writer, activist, and Holocaust survivor Elie Wiesel insisted, "We must take sides."[30]

The Forces of Influence diagram shows what humans do every day (see figure 1.2). First, we are influenced by the actions of others. Second, we consider that influence and then consult our values, attitudes, beliefs, and desires. Third, we act and influence others. And finally, we enjoy or suffer the consequences of our actions. And please note that consequences can be suspended or delayed for long periods of time. Swift and perfect justice is not a characteristic of this life.

It is helpful to understand that we go through this process every day of our lives. It's also critical to recognize that we have responsibility throughout the process.

- **You are responsible** for your own values, attitudes, beliefs, and desires. You have the final and only say in how you choose to be influenced by others.

- **You are responsible** for the actions you take and the influence you have on others. You have *moral agency*—the volition to make your own decisions about what's right and wrong.

Figure 1.2 The Forces of Influence

- **You are responsible** for the consequences of your actions and their influence on others, including how your actions affect other people's thoughts, feelings, beliefs, and choices.

You are responsible and accountable for what you think, feel, believe, say, and do. And you are responsible for the consequences. As Frederick Douglass said at the funeral of abolitionist William Lloyd Garrison, "It was the glory of this man that he could stand alone with the truth, and calmly await the result."[31]

The Three Scorpions

I have worked with law enforcement agencies at the federal, state, and local levels. I have trained leaders from the Secret Service; Federal Bureau of Investigation; Federal Drug Enforcement Agency; Bureau of Alcohol, Tobacco, Firearms and Explosives; and a host of other agencies. If you look at the data for ethical misconduct across these organizations, as well as state and local agencies, the pattern is the same. There are three primary categories of ethical misconduct:

- Lying, stealing, or cheating
- Substance abuse
- Sexual misconduct

We call these categories of ethical misconduct the *three scorpions*. What is fascinating is that the pattern is consistent over time, and, not surprisingly, the same pattern of misconduct applies to the rest of us. If you look at time-series data documenting law enforcement officer wrongdoing over the past 50 years, it's the same three scorpions. But that's not all that is predictable about the three scorpions; we also know what officers do to put themselves in a position to be stung. The pattern leading up to a sting is just as predictable as the sting itself. And what is it? It's simply the gradual deterioration of personal commitment to behave with integrity.

With few exceptions, officers begin their careers in a state of high commitment to their professional ethical standards. The most dangerous step for those who commit an ethical infraction is not the infraction itself but what we call the *first justification*. This refers to the first time the individual overrides an ethical standard by rationalizing it away.

A common initial infraction, for example, is violating a no-gratuity policy, which means accepting any gift, discount, or benefit one is offered by virtue of his or her profession. It's almost always a small thing such as accepting a free cup of coffee. It sounds absurd to many people, but what we find is that little missteps create little vulnerabilities. You accept one gratuity, then another, then another. And then one day, you have unsupervised access to confiscated property, and you know that the property was acquired with drug money. You rationalize and take some. That is how it happens.

Thankfully, not everyone is equally susceptible to the slippery slope from the point of first justification. When it comes to integrity, maintaining it has everything to do with sweating the small stuff. If you are vigilant and circumspect with the little things, you never reach the point of first justification. What is predictable is preventable. If you never allow yourself to cut a corner, preserving your integrity is absolutely predictable and engaging in ethical misconduct is absolutely preventable.

Principles of Integrity

Early in my career, I spent five years as the plant manager at Geneva Steel, the last remaining fully integrated steel plant west of the Mississippi River. The plant itself was an old relic built by United States Steel during World War II, with machinery sprawled across 2,000 acres. We ran the plant 24 hours a day, 365 days a year, shutting down only for scheduled maintenance. Of course I couldn't be there around-the-clock, so to cover more ground, connect with more people, and get my own sense of things, I made a habit of going on an occasional walkabout during swing and night shifts.

On one night's walkabout, I started at what we called the "hot end," making my way through the coke ovens and blast furnaces. The next stop was central maintenance. The people in central maintenance kept everything running; they were the electricians, pipefitters, millwrights, and other craft employees. It was about 2:00 a.m., and I wandered over to the break room near the electrical and machine shops. I opened the door. Pitch black.

I found the light switch and turned it on. Can you guess what I saw? That's right: 30 employees sound asleep on makeshift cots—and getting paid. I had a long, hefty flashlight in my hand and one question in my head: *Which end should I use?* Apparently with little compunction, these men (and they were all men) were sleeping on the job.

Every man caught sleeping that night was issued a formal reprimand and suspended from his job for a week. What was fascinating was the way the men responded individually. Some tried to hide behind the union and duck personal responsibility.

They went to great lengths to use the grievance procedure and formal arbitration not only to be cleared of wrongdoing but also to receive back pay for the time they were suspended. Other men took personal responsibility. They acknowledged their poor choice and wrote me letters of apology. Clearly, only the ones in the second category could look their children in the eyes and teach them about integrity.

Show Up and Follow Through

If integrity is basic honesty, a first principle is *Be honest with your time and effort.* I have a friend who has hired and managed thousands of people. I asked him this question: "What's the first principle of integrity?"

"Come to work," he said.

"That's it?" I asked.

"That's it. If you can be where you're supposed to be when you're supposed to be there, you have outperformed 25 percent of the human race."

"Is there a second principle?" I asked.

"There is: *follow through.* If you can follow through, in other words, do the work that you're assigned to do. And I'm not even saying that you do it well; but if you're trying, even though you are making mistakes, you have now outperformed 50 percent of the human race."

"So, you're saying that if you simply show up and follow through, you're in the top half of performance?"

"That's exactly what I'm saying," he replied. "It's the principle that Vince Lombardi taught the Green Bay Packers years ago: 'We're going to be brilliant on the basics.'[32] The ultimate basics are to show up and follow through. It's not easy to find people willing to do that."

If we are not passing this basic test of integrity by showing up and following through, chances are we're engaging in some form of self-deception, which is a low-cost way of self-medicating when we're not happy with our lives. But like all other illicit forms of pain avoidance, it does not make things better.

For many people the cost/benefit calculation is whether the costs of showing up and following through are higher than the short-term costs of not. We often choose self-deception because we have created a tolerable working accommodation with what we consider low-grade forms of dishonesty. It may bother us not to show up and follow through, but not enough to bring us to our feet. So, we convince ourselves that it won't matter, at least not today. We push it off. But as novelist, poet, and travel writer Robert Louis Stevenson is often quoted as having said, "Everybody, soon or late, sits down to a banquet of consequences."[33]

Human beings tend to change their behavior at the precipice. It takes a lot before the motivation to change is stronger than the motivation to stay the same. Inertia is a powerful force. And even when we do gain a sense of urgency to change, that urgency tends to be a catalyst and not a sustainer. Unfortunately, many people are crisis-activated.

If you think about it, not showing up and following through represents a pattern of avoiding effort. Integrity requires a consistent pattern of allocating effort. Infrequent bursts of effort are a clear indication of an integrity problem. In the final analysis, the act of showing up and following through is a gift of integrity we give ourselves and then give to others.

Help Others Have Integrity

In most organizations the ethical conduct of leaders follows a normal distribution curve. There are highly ethical employees at one end and highly unethical employees at the other. The rest of the population "occupy morally," as novelist and poet Thomas Hardy describes in *Far from the Madding Crowd,* "that vast middle space of Laodicean [half-hearted] neutrality which lay between the Sacrament people of the parish and the drunken division of its inhabitants."[34] What an organization and its leaders decide to do with that middle space often determines the organization's success.

An organization's ability to show integrity comes from uncompromising and deeply socialized values. It is a culture of ethical behavior that allows an organization to consistently keep its promises to its stakeholders over the long term, and keeping promises is the essence of high performance. Warren Buffett said, "Culture, more than rule books, determines how an organization behaves."[35]

When leaders get serious about competing on values, the organization gets serious about competing on values. It develops a fine-tuned moral sensitivity that becomes imbedded in the culture. Over time employees who do not agree or cannot abide the values leave. Meanwhile those who stay begin holding their leaders to a high standard of integrity. If they misstep, the employees will not wink.

Bob Moritz, the US chairman and a senior partner at PricewaterhouseCoopers, illustrates the point: "If I were to say something that appeared to conflict with PwC's stated values, it could go viral, and my credibility would be shot."[36] That is an incredibly good thing—a culture that holds its leaders accountable. How does it happen? It happens when leaders model ethical values long enough that those patterns of behavior become the prevailing norms of the organization.

The challenge today is that organizations recruit, hire, and onboard a higher percentage of employees who arrive with no moral compass, who do not self-govern, which makes the organization only as good as its control environment and system of corporate governance. Eventually, there is a breakdown in the system and a scandal on the way.

Protect Principles and Values

Think about this question: What is Google built on? The answer should give us clues about how desperately organizations need integrity. Of course, there is no perfect organization in the world, no complex adaptive enterprise that has the capacity to neutralize all competitive threats all the time. But Google is one of the best.

Is Google built on its proprietary technology—that original kernel of code developed by founders Larry Page and Sergey Brin that became Google's proprietary Internet search algorithm? Is it built on Google's mission to "organize the world's information and make it universally accessible and useful"? Is it built on Google's values as laid out in its Code of Conduct, at the core of which is the mantra *Don't be evil*?[37] The answer is yes. All three contribute to Google's success and competitive advantage. But there's an important issue here that relates to the useful life of these elements. At some point Google's current strategy will become fully amortized and have to change. And its mission? That could change, too, if Google decides to apply itself to other kinds of businesses. What about its values? Will it ever throw out *Don't be evil*? That would be catastrophic.

In early US history, we find a curious parallel between building a house then and building a modern organization today. When homesteaders pushed out the western frontier, they would find a fertile spot of land, build their homes, and settle until the prospect of better land, better conditions, and a brighter future appeared. Before they hitched their wagons and got back on the trail, they would burn their houses to reclaim the nails. The hand-forged nails were rare and valuable, a precious asset they could not afford to leave behind.

Regardless of the brilliance of your strategy, the magnetism of your vision, the soundness of your execution, and the intimacy of your customer service, next to the inherent worth of human beings, a company's principles and values are its most precious asset. In time everything else will be discarded. Inevitably, strategy will reach the end of its useful life. How you create and deliver value will change, as well as all the scaffolding that supports it. Your systems, structure, processes, practices, roles, responsibilities, and technology are configurable parts. It's all perishable, with one exception: fixed principles and core values. They must stay.

Principles and values are the basis of making and keeping promises to employees and customers. They provide assurance, confidence, and trust out of predictive understanding.[38] They are the last and enduring source of value. When they go, everything goes. When an organization abandons its principles and values, it removes its moral infrastructure and collapses under its own weight. Too many leaders and too many organizations are compelled to "learn geology the morning after the earthquake," as poet and essayist Ralph Waldo Emerson once noted.[39] The epitaphs of many failed organizations read *Died of self-inflicted wounds* because everything was negotiable.

Nothing about an organization's strategy or business model is sacrosanct. But there must be a cutting point between principles and values and everything else. They represent precious, freestanding assets that must be independent of strategy. They provide continuity and identity when everything else is expendable. They represent the core element of the culture and the unchanging soul of the organization.

Cases in which leaders have successfully remodeled an entire enterprise represent organizational change in its comprehensive and supreme category. We learn from these cases that retaining principles and values during the process of change is not only possible but necessary to provide an anchor. Ironically, perhaps, organizations with the strongest principles and values often have the highest adaptive capacity because people attach themselves to them and understand that everything else is on the table. If you want to keep your promises, burn the house when it's time to reinvent the company. But save the nails.

INTEGRITY: SUMMARY POINTS

Society is immoral in its feigned attempts to be amoral.

We have an integrity problem because the triangle of socialization is broken and we have embraced moral relativism.

You will constantly be tempted to engage in ethical misconduct.

Integrity depends on fixed principles and moral values.

Model, teach, and defend integrity. You cannot be neutral.

You are responsible for:

- ◆ *Your values, attitudes, beliefs, and desires*
- ◆ *Your actions and influence*
- ◆ *The consequences of your actions and influence*

To avoid the slippery slope, avoid the first justification.

Be consistent in showing up and following through.

Creating a culture of integrity allows the organization to keep its promises.

When it's time to abandon your strategy, do not abandon your principles and core values.

Integrity is a source of personal and organizational competitive advantage in the twenty-first century.

CHAPTER 2

The Second Cornerstone of Character:

Humility

[The highest level of leadership] builds
enduring greatness through a paradoxical blend
of personal humility and professional will.

James C. "Jim" Collins (1958–)
American business consultant, lecturer, and author
Good to Great (2001)

Does Humility Really Matter?

The second cornerstone of character is humility. People will tell you politely that humility is important, but most don't really believe it. As an attribute, humility has a weak public reputation and a bad name. People think it's soft, cowering, and acquiescent when in fact the opposite is true. So my first job is to puncture that myth. The bottom line is that humility is a performance accelerator. It allows you to develop, grow, and progress faster. This unadorned attribute is shockingly powerful. Ironically, it is also one of the most difficult to cultivate.

In his autobiography Benjamin Franklin said, "In reality, there is, perhaps, no one of our natural passions so hard to subdue as pride. Disguise it, struggle with it, beat it down, stifle it, mortify it as much as one pleases, it is still alive, and will every now and then peep out and show itself; you will see it, perhaps, often in this history; for, even if I could conceive that I had completely overcome it, I should probably be proud of my humility."[1]

Let me define *humility* and then tell you why it matters so much. Humility, which is an extension of integrity, is the capacity to withstand the truth of your own dependency and ignorance. It's the grateful and unresented acceptance that you don't know much and can't do much without help. Arrogance, on the other hand, is an occupational hazard. It can lead to impaired judgment and poor decision-making.

We depend on one another. In a strict sense, there is no such thing as purely personal accomplishment, especially in an organizational setting. Humility not only acknowledges the brute fact of your own dependency but also includes a fitting sense of gratitude. That sense of gratitude is a safeguard, a check on ego and its inherent dangers.[2] As Kevin Sharer, the former CEO of biotech firm Amgen, put it, "There is a price to be paid for arrogance."[3] The liability exposure of an arrogant leader is enormous. Why is it dangerous to feel superior, overconfident, or smug? Why is the littleness of vanity not little?

- Humble leaders accept reality, whereas arrogant leaders often create new versions that make them look important when things are going well and that hold them harmless when things are going south.

- Humble leaders are poised in receiving bad news, while arrogant leaders are punitive.

- Humble leaders embrace and participate in a rigorous contest of ideas. They encourage questions and give people permission to challenge the status quo. Arrogant leaders see questions as a challenge to their authority, status, and the current distribution of power.[4]

- Humble leaders reflect; arrogant leaders deflect.

- Humble leaders grow; arrogant leaders swell.

- Humble leaders value contribution over competition; arrogant leaders value competition over contribution.

In the twenty-first century, humility will become an increasing source of enduring competitive advantage because we are working in a dynamic and unforgiving context. To succeed both personally and professionally, you must remain open and submissive to reality.[5]

Sometimes you will have the vision and perception to be preemptive. At other times, no matter how anticipatory you try to be, you will find yourself reacting and responding to threats you did not see coming. To be open and stay open, you will need the intellectual, emotional, and spiritual quality that is humility. How do you cultivate and maintain humility? You must be willing to confront your own failures, mistakes, and weaknesses. This will require a steady diet of undiluted feedback and continual striving for self-awareness.

Finally, humility matters because it strips you of self-centeredness, allowing you to influence others with more-penetrating persuasion. It removes the scales of prejudice from your eyes so that you can see more clearly. It gives you a greater desire to know people—their stories, their trials and triumphs, their heartaches and aspirations. With humility you are much more likely to act with poise and patience under pressure and less likely to be frustrated, get angry, and show signs of compassion fatigue. Humility purifies your intent and burns out ulterior motives. You well up with love and a desire to serve. People sense this and become more responsive to your influence. They will work harder and contribute more because they know that you esteem and value them.

What Is Your Tolerance for Candor?

When I coach executives, one of the first things I try to assess is their humility. To do this, I ask them a question: "On a scale from 1 to 10, where 1 is low and 10 is high, what is your tolerance for candor?" And then I say, "Don't answer the question now. Go home and think about it. Do some soul-searching. You have a week. Then let's talk." No one has ever given him- or herself a 10.

Developing a high tolerance for candor is a sign of humility that translates into high performance. The writer of Proverbs understood this: "He that refuseth instruction despiseth his own soul: but he that heareth reproof getteth understanding."[6] Developing a tolerance for candor is a matter of both skill and will—both the ability as well as the desire.

Arrogance and hubris create a reality distortion field. They tempt you to create a fictional account of your life and your performance, and that tendency spills over into your relationships and the organization. Leaders with a low tolerance for candor consider straight feedback a form of trespassing. They protect their egos and their status by punishing those who want to speak truth to power. If you can overcome the natural human impulse to get defensive, you will accelerate as a leader.

Narinder Singh, CEO of Topcoder, said in an interview:

> The leaders I've admired the most over the years weren't afraid of being challenged. Some people say they want to be challenged, but they want to be challenged only in a way that makes them look like the smartest person in the room. That was off-putting for me, and I wanted to make sure people never felt that way dealing with me. If I have somebody working for me who's really good, I should lose 80 percent of the arguments I have with them because they should know their area better than I do. People have to feel that the best idea wins.[7]

Get yourself to a place where you can take it straight. Ask for direct and candid feedback from a different person every day for 10 days. This will arrest your ego and put you in a humble state of mind. Once you develop a taste for reality, you will want more. It will become your diet, and you'll never want it filtered again.

But humility goes beyond receiving candid feedback. It means you are willing to be corrected and to act on that correction. It means you're prepared to be wrong. You're willing to let others evaluate—and perhaps even plumb the depths of your performance—because you understand that the journey of personal development cannot be traveled alone. You have learned through observation and experience that there must be honesty from the inside and candor from the outside. Without it we stumble over ourselves. We get stupid because we are suffering from isolation.

Your first obligation is to have a truthful encounter with reality. But you cannot do that alone. For the humble, feedback, as the chalkboard aphorism goes, really is the breakfast of champions. Author, poet, and philosopher Henry David Thoreau observed, "It is as hard to see oneself as to look backwards without turning round."[8] I am inclined to agree because I observe many leaders who don't ponder their performance.

Leaders who lack humility are generally insecure, which makes them dodgy and impenetrable. They don't want to touch the cold stone of reality. They bristle at unvarnished feedback. They are too sure of themselves to listen. There are talents and there are self-perceived talents. Arrogant people do not know the difference. They tend to travel down avenues of self-importance and self-doubt. They want to be the only noodle in the soup, and they want others to be their lapdogs of validation.

Arrogant people refuse to acknowledge that there are others all around them who are wise in perception and have the precious gift of guidance to give. They cannot bear the thought of bad press. They prefer polite society, cocktail-party talk, fulsome praise, and fabled reality. Candor? The juice is not worth the squeeze.

Humility can be the single most important factor that separates good leaders from great ones. Often the greater the success a leader has, the more unwilling he is to receive guidance and direction. Executives, in particular, frequently believe that they have graduated from the ranks of the learner. And that belief is often the insurmountable obstacle that separates them from achieving their true potential. In soliciting feedback for his books, for example, one prominent author emphasizes the importance of getting honest, high-quality feedback: "What I really want is for them to tell me where the problems are....You need nonsycophantic people who will tell you the truth."[9] But who is going to do that if you're not humble?

Humility is not just teachability; it's not just a willingness to learn. It is a willingness to unlearn and change. Humility is a willingness to accept feedback; acknowledge faults, limitations, and deficiencies; and then act with determination to improve. Leadership is a process of self-discovery, but it must be aided self-discovery. We all have blind spots that can seriously impair our performance. Or we may have glaring weaknesses that we cannot overcome on our own. You may recall that King George VI ascended the British throne after the sudden abdication of his brother. Thankfully, the monarch was humble enough to seek out help for his debilitating speech impediment. That mixture of humility and courage was a key to his success.

In his masterpiece "Recessional," poet and novelist Rudyard Kipling expresses the pride and regret that attend a nation's rise and fall. Kipling could see that Victorian England would fall into inevitable decline, yet he was not mourning the loss of empire but a more serious loss—that of humility:

> The tumult and the shouting dies;
> The Captains and the Kings depart:

> Still stands Thine ancient sacrifice,
> An humble and a contrite heart.
> Lord God of Hosts, be with us yet,
> Lest we forget—lest we forget!"[10]

If a leader constantly cultivates humility, it eventually allows him to transition to a more evolved stage of development: the final stage of confidence.

The Final Stage of Confidence

The *final stage of confidence* is a term I use to describe the culminating phase of a leader's character development. More than anything else, it is a measure of humility and the conquest of ego. It's a stage not many leaders attain, though everyone has the opportunity. It's a hard place to get to, especially if you have a track record of high achievement that suggests you know what you're doing. Business theorist Chris Argyris wrote, "Because many professionals are almost always successful at what they do, they rarely experience failure. And because they have rarely failed, they have never learned how to learn from failure. So whenever their single-loop learning strategies go wrong, they become defensive, screen out criticism, and put the 'blame' on anyone and everyone but themselves. In short, their ability to learn shuts down precisely at the moment they need it the most."[11]

Clearly, it's harder for some people to reach this stage, depending on how the mix of natural endowment, circumstance, and choice comes together. But even the most disadvantaged people can reach the final stage of confidence because the third factor—choice—is the determining one, and over time it has the ability to outstrip and overcome the influences of the other two. It really is a choice.

If you have ever come in contact with a leader who has reached the final stage of confidence, you may not remember it. The interaction may have left no lasting impression. In fact, that would not be surprising because final-stage leaders are people who have transitioned from the impulse to impress to the higher impulse to bless. It's not important to them that you remember them.

Let me describe some of the common behavioral characteristics of leaders in the final stage of confidence. These traits are not tied to a particular personality type, level of intelligence, or style. Final-stage leaders do tend to become more interpersonally similar, however, in the outward expressions of the inward humility they share.

Final-stage leaders have made peace with themselves. They have subdued their egos. That fact comes out prominently in their behavior. Final-stage leaders are far less prone to engage in flattery, self-promotion, and attention-getting behavior. Here are a few observable patterns in final-stage leaders:

- They don't need to hear themselves talk, so they don't clamor for airtime. They stop telling the world how smart they are.

- They don't seek status through association, so they refrain from dropping names.

- They don't subscribe to the leader-as-expert model in which the leader is the repository of all knowledge. As a result, they become more content to listen and ask questions rather than talk and tell.

- They value the appreciation and recognition of their peers when it's meaningful, but it's not a requirement. They have learned that leadership often requires that we go for long periods and long distances without reward or recognition, that we toil in obscurity, and that due credit might come, but it might not. Final-stage leaders learn to fuel their efforts through intrinsic rewards. They learn that achievement carries its own compensation.

■ At the same time, final-stage leaders don't deflect recognition with false modesty. They are not coy or demure. They are grateful for accurate and deserved recognition.

■ They correct others faster and with more candor, but feedback is given in the spirit of empathy and real concern.

■ They praise genuinely and specifically, not gratuitously. Leaders who have not reached the final stage of confidence often praise either profusely to be seen as generous or sparingly out of resentment, or because they believe praise to be a scarce resource.

■ They are less hurt and less provoked by the careless and mean-spirited acts of others. In one case, I repeatedly observed an arrogant leader cutting off a final-stage leader in a group discussion. The arrogant leader was attempting to establish dominance with tiresome alpha-male behavior, while the final-stage leader patiently deferred. Everyone rolled their eyes.

■ Final-stage leaders become more kind and yet more demanding at the same time. They delegate more with the understanding that people grow only when they stretch. They realize that stretching is both painful and exhilarating and that it's the only place new capacity is built.

It is a blessed day when a leader crosses the threshold to the final stage of confidence. Until then the journey toward deeper humility, and what one observer called "the lower levels of meekness,"[12] will influence a leader's behavior in many ways.

Humility and the Mundane

Here is another key to cultivating humility: do mundane work, or what some people call stoop labor. It's an antidote to pride. It reduces the chance that you'll be victimized by affluence. Hang on to the stoop labor, even if it's simply washing the dishes. It keeps you grounded. Whether at work, school, or home, take the opportunity to do some of the monotonous, mundane, prosaic, and most likely unappreciated work that has to get done in this world. It always seems to generate humility as a by-product. Take my oldest son, for example. One summer when he was in high school, he worked as a busboy at a restaurant. Who knew this lowly job could yield such rich dividends?

In a remarkable way, the hours he spent clearing, cleaning, washing, and stocking taught him lessons I could not. That unskilled and unheralded post that sits at the bottom of the food chain, that lowest rung on the labor-force ladder, that microcosm of the human condition, became a cherished teacher. And that teacher taught him, not always lovingly but nonetheless effectively, the reality of people and organizations—engagement, performance, and follow-through; time and resource constraints; quality, costs, and productivity; throughput, customer service, and process flow; power and politics; fairness and discrimination; greed and servant leadership—all in a way I never could. For minimum wage you get a full curriculum—if you're paying attention.

One night he came home at midnight after a shift. We got to talking in the kitchen, and it turned into a spontaneous debrief. He had that look of tired satisfaction on his face that you get when you have worked hard at something and you feel simultaneously exhausted and exhilarated. He smelled like barbecue. I asked him what lessons he had learned on the job. I got out a piece of paper and captured the lessons:

- I define my own work ethic. Some employees try to see what they can get away with. They shirk the work. If you can leave a mountain of dishes for the next guy, do it. Others work hard and do not look for shortcuts. It's up to you.

- Praise goes up, and complaints go down. Insecure people tend to hoard praise and deflect complaints. Confident people value complaints as learning opportunities.

- Visibility creates opportunity. We tip the server, not the busboy. I didn't get too many tips.

- People don't always treat people like people. Unskilled labor is simply expected and not normally appreciated. The busboy works in the shadows. The summons by a customer, "Hey, busboy," is the ultimate reminder that most people consider busboys commoditized flesh.

- I have a new appreciation for the value of the dollar. Working as a busboy teaches you to look at the price of everything in terms of hours worked. If I want to buy something, I ask myself if it's really worth the money. I have learned to be more frugal and to spend more carefully.

- The boss sets the tone. It can range from pathetic to inspiring. Some bosses follow a say-and-do-not principle. One boss, for instance, prior to the dinner rush would yell at everybody to get going and then go sit in his car to have a smoke. Another boss would get to work and say almost nothing, and people would follow his example.

- Smile when people are rude. Unfortunately, customers often have a hard time being nice. In the course of a shift, you will encounter the full spectrum of customer behavior, ranging from the very rude to the very gracious. When someone pegs out the rudeness meter, smile, do your best and be happy you don't have to go home with that person.

- Small gestures go a long way. Why is it that there is so much power in a simple "thank you"? But there is.

- It's good to lose your ego. No task is beneath you. I fill the dumpster with trash, scrub the floor, and then punch my card and go home. You get over yourself pretty quickly.

- This job is not a destination. It's been great. I have learned a lot. But suddenly I've become very motivated to stay in school.

It has been my privilege to work alongside each of our children, scrubbing pots and pans and mopping the floor. You cannot automate the kind of connection and talk time that has come from all that kitchen labor over the years. One day my son and I made major repairs to a toilet. As a result, we can both recite the internal anatomy of a toilet tank, something neither of us aspired to learn. We stooped for a few hours together, interspersed with trips to the hardware store. When we finally pulled the lever and saw the bowl fill with water, it was musical. I earned credibility with my son, and we both gained a bit of confidence in our practical and glorious triumph.

After my first year of graduate school, I didn't have enough money to pay tuition for the next semester. A friend of mine invited me to work with him in the vineyards near Bakersfield, California. The stoop labor allowed me to stay in school. As I worked alongside the migrant laborers, I learned once again that I am no better than anyone else.

People gain confidence through concentrated effort. If you can't sustain focus, you can seldom accomplish meaningful goals.[13] For example, my wife and I are do-it-yourselfers in the yard instead of hiring out the work. We have generously handed down this tradition to our sons and daughters. With the spring thaw each year, our children begin issuing advance warnings, alerting us to the fact that they will not be pulling weeds this year. I smile back and tell them that the Clark family is not a democracy. If my kids can weed for few hours straight, I know they have the capacity to do their homework, learn an instrument, help a neighbor, and stay focused at choir or basketball practice.

Mundane labor has a magical way of removing the feeling that self is the center of life. There's another ennobling thing that happens when we engage in stoop labor: we retain more mental, emotional, and physical agility. This has come in handy for those who have suffered job loss or economic reversal. When people lose their jobs, for example, they often expect to find new jobs at or near the same level of responsibility and income. What if they can't? Some people cannot face this, and it breaks them. If you are humble, you're more willing to bend and do what you can, like a friend of mine who as a seasoned professional had to stock shelves at Walmart to feed his family. Emotionally, he was set back, but with humility he recovered. Eventually, he got a better job. It was through humility that he was willing to swallow his pride, overcome his financial reversal, and claim the victory.

Humility and Your Motivation to Achieve

I have a cowboy friend who competes in rodeos. If he wins an event, he brings home an enormous belt buckle. I'm not quite sure why anyone would want to wear a piece of hardware like that, but make no mistake, these are highly coveted items. An oft-quoted maxim of Napoleon's is "A soldier will fight long and hard for a bit of colored ribbon." Cowboys will fight even harder for one of these platter-size belt buckles.

There is a large body of research that highlights the short span of extrinsic motivation—meaning motivation that comes from the outside. We know that rewards motivate, so we sometimes assume that more rewards motivate more. Not true. There is a steep curve of diminishing returns in which people hit a saturation point. A few cowboy belt buckles may be a good thing, but at some point you just put them in a drawer. So, what's the proper motivation to achieve? Here are a couple of observations.

Avoid overachievement. The motivation to achieve should not be confused with the high-need-for-achievement disorder, which is an unhealthy addiction in some people. For people afflicted with this malady, achievement does not bring the normal rewards. Rather, it brings "relief in the accomplishment of tasks," as writer Kim Girard observes. "Moving immediately to the next task on the list, they [individuals] never savor accomplishments for long....This creates a vicious cycle marked by a feeling of little or no real sense of purpose and a 'flatness'—in career and life."[14] This cycle is based on achieving for the wrong reasons, and it results in serious imbalance.

Achievement can become a very selfish activity, driven by ego or insecurity, in which a person obsesses on building a résumé of accomplishment as a means of showcasing oneself. In this case as well, the motivation is off the mark.

Achievement is a moral obligation. The final-stage leader develops gifts and potential for personal enjoyment, fulfillment, and the service of others.

Avoid entitlement. There is a maxim that says, *If you want what you never had, you must do what you have never done.* There's a huge strain of entitlement in our society. Many people prefer leisure to performance, and security to risk-taking. Entitlement is the beguilement of low expectations. It's the treachery of believing that you can violate the principle of work and still achieve something worthwhile. David Starr Jordan, the founding president of Stanford University, made this point clear: "What is worth having comes at the cost which corresponds to its worth."[15] Society has a tendency to turn luxuries into necessities, and necessities into rights. For example, I have to remind my teenagers that owning a smartphone is not in the Bill of Rights. Entitlement is an imitation of the real principle of achievement and an inversion of truth.

Another common masquerade for genuine achievement is to rely on connections and credentials instead of character, competence, and real effort. If you are less willing to sacrifice, you're easily seduced by alternative routes to success. This wrongful thinking can lead to ethical misconduct. It's easier to grease a palm or enter an unholy alliance than to get out there and sweat your way to a goal. Once the seed of entitlement sprouts, it begins to crowd out initiative and healthy ambition. You start telling yourself that effort really isn't the source of success, so you go looking for substitutes.

Communicate with Humility

The communication paradigm of a humble leader is one that values understanding. Humble leaders are just as determined to boldly advocate and motivate, but they do it differently—they do it without calling attention to themselves.

Unfortunately, too many of us have been taught that to get ahead we need to obsess on the care and feeding of our personal brand and the cultivation of an elusive quality that people call "executive presence." These ideas have done untold damage to individuals, organizations, and the very concept of leadership. Here's a sample of what it means to achieve this rarefied state of awesomeness: *executive presence* relates to the ability to command a room, display gravitas, set an authoritative tone of voice, project magnetism, and exhibit a host of other stylistics.

Those traits can be praiseworthy, but they're not essential. What if you don't have smooth, unflappable poise? What if you're not straight out of central casting, not gregarious, and, quite frankly, not very good at public speaking? Are you at risk as a leader?

In the business world especially, we tend to worship at the altar of platform skills and rhetorical bling while often missing the more important issue of *intent*. Here is the paradox: I see angular, fumbling, scattered, and interpersonally clumsy leaders succeed in communicating effectively with their people—not because they are great communicators but because they speak directly to listener need out of a deep and transparent commitment for the concerns of other people. On the other hand, I also see polished and talented leaders cause a collective stupor when they open their mouths.

When we think about leadership, we may be overconditioned to look at the skills side of the equation. We may label as a skill barrier what is in fact a deficiency that resides in a deeper place—the place of intent. The implication is simple and yet profound: If you lack humility, all the skill development in the world will amount to nothing but window dressing. If your primary intent is to look good rather than be understood, you have it backward. More skill can't solve the problem. It's the wrong corrective action for the root cause. Technique and stylistics will not get it done.

Here are a few suggestions.

Show up as a giver. When you approach people to communicate with them, assess your intent. Are you preoccupied with yourself? If you are unencumbered by self-interest, your message will travel with greater velocity and impact to the hearts and minds of those you lead. You will have more social capital to spend because you are earning more through the motivation to serve instead of the motivation to shine.

Meet people where they are. Do not make people come to you. Reach out to greet them at their cognitive, emotional, and cultural starting points.[16] Reflect deeply on what they care about. It will magnify your reach and effect because you have anticipated and can therefore speak more directly to the questions and challenges people have.

De-emphasize yourself. Especially if you happen to hold a fancy title, de-emphasize yourself, not in role or commitment but in importance. In other words, eliminate those aspects of content and delivery that unnecessarily draw attention to you personally and therefore away from the substance of what you say. This is strong medicine for leaders who are struggling to change themselves from personal brand managers into better leaders. Rather than worry about the nursing of your image, ration your publicity. It goes back to the job you are commissioned to do—a job that must be powered by the trust and confidence you create in those you lead.

Use simple language. Simple language refers to words and phrases that don't need to be translated to be understood. Using simple language is a particular challenge for well-educated, insecure leaders who feel an unguided impulse to impress others with technical or business jargon. For example, it builds more intellectual understanding and emotional support if you say, "If we work together, we'll get better results," rather than, "If we leverage our synergies through collaborative effort, the value-add will make us more successful." There's way too much swelling business-speak out there. The goal is to make yourself impossible to be misunderstood in both content and intent.

Again, strive to teach, align, and motivate. Jack Welch, former CEO of General Electric, said it well: "Self-confident people don't need to wrap themselves in complexity and all that clutter that passes for sophistication in business. Self-confident leaders produce simple plans, speak simply and propose big, clear targets."[17]

HUMILITY: SUMMARY POINTS

Humility is the capacity to withstand the truth of your dependency and ignorance.

Reflect and grow rather than deflect and swell.

Purify your intent with humility to influence others with greater credibility, persuasion, and love.

Avoid arrogance and the reality distortion field it creates.

Develop a high tolerance for candor and promote that in your culture.

Prepare to be wrong. Be willing to unlearn and change.

Strive to reach the final stage of confidence and lose the preoccupation with self.

Engage in mundane labor to stay grounded and humble, and encourage others to do the same.

Avoid the traps of overachievement and entitlement.

Communicate with the intent to be understood, not to draw attention to yourself.

CHAPTER 3

The Third Cornerstone of Character:

Accountability

*The key to your happiness is to own your
own slippers, own who you are, own how you look,
own your family, own the talents you have, and own the
ones you don't. If you keep saying your slippers aren't
yours, then you'll die searching, you'll die bitter, always
feeling you were promised more. Not only our actions,
but also our omissions, become our destiny.*

Abraham Verghese (1955–)
Physician, professor of medicine at Stanford University, and author
Cutting for Stone (2009)

Will You Hold Yourself Accountable?

The third cornerstone of character is personal accountability. A leader must demand accountability of himself. Go back with me to 1783 and let me introduce you to the most accountable man of his generation.

It's a cold December day. You are standing in a crowded public gallery. Suddenly, your eyes meet the image of a stately figure entering the chamber. Silence ordered, this man of commanding presence bows, delivers a short speech, and then pulls from his military dress uniform a document and hands it to the ranking official. The visitor turns to face what has become a sea of swollen eyes and watery cheeks. He bows again, waves farewell, and then rides off to have Christmas dinner with his family.

The place? Annapolis, Maryland. The setting? The US Continental Congress. The man? General George Washington. What just happened? You have just witnessed one of the most breathtaking acts of accountability in all of human history. The most powerful man on earth walked into the room—a man who strapped a fledgling nation to his back and led a ragamuffin army every day for six years, who waged war with the most formidable fighting force on the planet and won. On that particular day, more than two centuries ago, the question on everyone's mind was: *What will this man do next?* What *should* he do next?

In real terms, the general possessed absolute power. If he should make himself king of the new nation, it would be a very natural act, and it would be what every ruler of the day expected him to do. He could wear the crown. He could ascend the throne. But this man of quiet reserve, the tall farmer from Virginia, did something more astonishing: he walked away. In a precedent-setting act that reverberates to this day, this titan of the times held himself accountable. Rather than abuse power, he voluntarily laid down his commission as commander in chief. He stunned the world and went home. Can you picture him riding off to Mount Vernon? He would not even accept pay for his service during the war, just reimbursement for his expenses.

In this episode and in many others from his life, Washington taught us that leadership is not about the leader. It's not about being made king of anything. In reality, it's mostly about the quiet, mundane, and intensely human things of everyday life, sprinkled with heroics here and there. And it's about being accountable for your actions.

In feats of daring, the general crossed the Delaware River to mount a surprise attack on a garrison at Trenton, New Jersey.

He also made dreadful mistakes along the way.[1] But he would not quit. In the end he laid siege to the British at Yorktown and forced General Charles Cornwallis to surrender. But most of the time, he spent his days doing very unheroic things like keeping the troops warm and fed and persuading them not to go home.

There will always be a march of folly, a procession of leaders who misbehave because they believe they are accountable to no one. They are not leading to serve; they are leading to self-serve. The ancient Greek dramatist Sophocles hit it on the head when he said,

> But hard it is to learn
> The mind of any mortal or the heart,
> Till he be tried in chief authority.
> Power shows the man.[2]

If you can hold yourself accountable in power, you have passed a test few men and women have the character to achieve.

Stanford professor Jeffrey Pfeffer explains how power has a tendency to melt away one's sense of personal accountability. "Research shows," he explains, "that people with more power tend to pay less attention to others. They are more action-oriented, pursue their own goals, and exhibit disinhibited behavior in part because they believe that rules don't apply to them; they are special and invulnerable."[3]

There Is No Such Thing as Hiding

Like Washington, all great leaders share the attribute of personal accountability. They privately self-correct even if others do not. How do you get to that point? First, you have to eliminate the three primary patterns of deflection in which humans tend to engage (see figure 3.1):

- ■ **Denial.** Denying is the act of refusing to acknowledge the truth.

Figure 3.1 The Patterns of Deflection

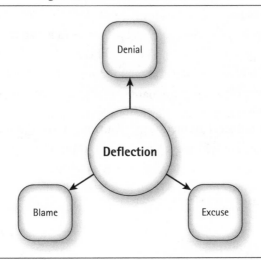

- **Blame.** Blaming is the act of transferring responsibility to someone else or something else.

- **Excuse.** Excusing is the act of justifying your actions based on something outside your control that relieves you of the burden of responsibility.

Patterns of deflection have one thing in common: They are attempts to avoid accountability. They are attempts to hide. Deflection simply blocks progress. If you deflect, you're stuck. If you hold yourself accountable, you move forward.

After high school I went to Brigham Young University on an NCAA football scholarship. The prospect of playing Division I football was exciting, but what lay ahead was a grueling journey. When I arrived on campus for summer camp, I didn't realize that over the subsequent 30 days I would sweat away the equivalent of my body weight. Even more chilling was the realization that I was taking an upper-division physics course, but it was applied as opposed to theoretical physics. I reflected on Newton's second law of motion:

force = mass × acceleration

I had entered a megaton realm in which the human species ran a whole lot faster and hit a whole lot harder.

Soon after I arrived, I walked across the practice field and noticed a tall steel-framed tower. Curious, I asked a teammate what it was. He told me it was a video tower and proceeded to explain that at the college level they film football practices. That was a new concept for me. In high school they filmed games but never practices. About two weeks later, I was sitting in a meeting with the other defensive linemen when the coach chastised me for allowing the offense to run around my side earlier in practice.

"Clark, you lost containment three times. You can't let the offensive lineman turn you inside. You've got to get off the ball and control the corner."

"But, Coach," I protested, "I only lost containment once."

A hush fell over the room. All heads swiveled in my direction. I met the sharp glance of my coach, who uttered seven fateful words: "The eye in the sky never lies." He turned to the white screen in front of the room and pushed the play button on the remote. There in living color, before the living and the dead, was Mr. Meat Squad, freshman Clark, losing containment—not once, not twice, but three times.

That experience left an imprint on my life. There are some activities that are performed in environments of total transparency. Football is one of those. Unfortunately, leadership is not, and therefore the journey to complete and self-directed accountability can be painful. Leadership is mostly exercised within the private chambers of our own lives. It's easy to deflect. Business is this way, politics even more so. The lack of transparency—this inability for all to see clear, cause-and-effect relationships and be answerable for them—has a tendency to encourage the three forms of deflection: denying, blaming, and excusing. You cannot do that if the performance environment is transparent. The very concept of hiding does not exist.

I am grateful for that defining day when I had to shed my bluster and bravado, my insecurity and my unreality, and was forced to have a truthful encounter with my own performance. What a priceless lesson. In many cases, we see leaders who succeed only because they don't visibly fail. There's no eye in the sky. They talk while nothing really substantive happens. Or they simply conceal their mistakes or incompetency from view and hide in the bowels of the organization. A lot of people hide and get away with it. They nestle into their organizations and live out sheltered professional lives in cocoons of job security, courtesy of incumbency, complexity, and ambiguity. We need to remind ourselves that we are all accountable, even if there is no one to push the play button or turn on the lights. Great leaders do. They hold themselves accountable—especially in the dark.

The Progression of Personal Accountability

If you are willing to hold yourself accountable, you will find that you naturally progress through three levels of personal account-ability: task, project/process, and outcome (see figure 3.2).

Task Accountability

The first level of accountability is the task level. When I assign my son Ben to cut the grass, I am giving him a *task*—a basic, discrete, and divisible unit of work. Everything we do, we do at the task level. This is the level of getting things done and of living life. If you accomplish the tasks that are most important today, you are successful. How do you approach a week? In exactly the same

Figure 3.2 The Three Levels of Accountability

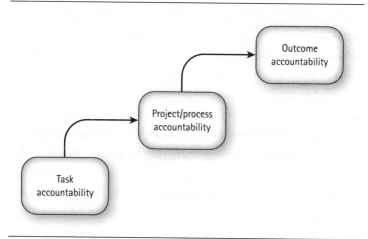

way. How about a month or year? It's the same. It never changes. You can think and plan in broader terms and at a higher altitude, but you can act only at the task level in the moment. It's the basic curriculum for becoming a successful person.

Project/Process Accountability

When you consistently demonstrate the ability to perform at the task level of accountability, it's time to graduate to the *project/ process* level—the ability to perform a set of related tasks with a given scope, a timeline, parameters, and objectives. *Projects* are clusters of tasks that have specific objectives, as well as a begin-ning and an end. A *process* is a string of tasks that are put together in a deliberate sequence to accomplish a repeating objective. Now I say to my son Ben, "Cut, trim, water, and fertilize the grass." Ben gains more responsibility and more autonomy at the same time. The risk goes up as does the reward. It's the only way Ben can progress.

Outcome Accountability

Now comes the big transition and the big test: taking on outcome accountability. At this level we do not prescribe the tasks, tools, or process. We simply say, "This is the outcome we're looking for." For my son it goes like this: "Ben, I want a manicured yard. Make it happen!" If you want to progress to your full potential as a leader, you have to take the leap to outcome accountability. This is your final graduation to the highest level of accountability. *Outcome* accountability is where the magic happens because this is where autonomy, creativity, and independence are given their full expression; it unleashes enormous power because you own the process. If you have to figure something out, you are more likely to accept inner responsibility for the results. You can make it your own.

"Social scientists have determined," writes psychology professor Robert Cialdini, "that we accept inner responsibility for a behavior when we think we have chosen to perform it in the absence of strong outside pressures."[4]

Starting versus Finishing

Accountability means finishing. Starting is the easy part. It's easy to start things. Start exercising. Start school. Start waking up earlier. Start being nicer. It's easy to start serving others or really listen to someone—at least for a day. It's not so easy the second day. The grade gets steeper and it doesn't level out until you've incorporated the change into your personal behavior.

Because the shelf-life of emotion is short, finishing becomes the exception. Look around and you soon notice the pattern of things that started well and ended poorly. People and the organizations they build are littered with the failed remains of false starts. In statistics it's called a *regression to the mean,* and it represents the dominant failure pattern (see figure 3.3).

Figure 3.3 Regression to the Mean

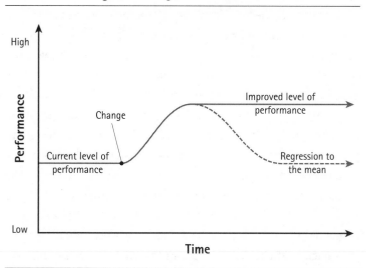

But in the wreckage we find insight. It becomes obvious that we simply take our hands off the wheel too soon. We declare victory or we get tired, bored, or distracted. And then we fall back. It happens over and over. Sometimes we learn from our failures, but it usually takes a while to really find the desire and discipline to be a finisher, to be accountable, to go the distance. The act of completion comes from the inside. When the lights go down and the crowds disperse, you're on your own. And that's usually what finishing is all about. It's lonely, inglorious work. It's private accountability in the dark. If you feed on praise and recognition, finishing is hard. Why finish when you can seek out new company and move on to something new?

Think about finishing in organizations. Think about the perverse incentives that tempt leaders to throw in the towel prematurely. Starting is fun—it's where the instant gratification is. It's where most human resource management systems provide reinforcement. Finishing is different. Finishing is the steep ascent, the lonely road, the long, hard slog. Finishing is done in obscurity. The incentives have dried up. The thrill is gone. It comes down to grinding discipline, often when no one cares. Finally, we often mistake momentum for completion, so we think we are done. That is when we have a regression to the mean.

Installing a new software system is the classic case here. Company A installs a new system, managers train everyone to use it, and during the first few weeks it's rocky and painful. The system is new, people are not used to it, and there are bugs. The employees are doing their part, but that does not mean they like it, embrace it, or would use it if they had a choice. They are only behaviorally compliant. Sure enough, a few weeks later everyone goes back to the legacy system, and the new software initiative becomes an expensive sunk cost. The leaders did not go the distance. They took their hands off the wheel. They did not capture hearts and minds. People never got onboard.

What does it take to be a strong finisher? It takes a person whose capacity to endure planned deprivation is stronger than the desire for instant gratification. To finish is to endeavor for a greater reward. Does that sound like something our society would espouse? That is part of the problem. Increasingly, our popular culture has reproach and merry disdain for the values that lead to finishing, and nothing but vulgar, narcissistic adoration for the values that lead to starting. Society seems to teach us less and less about finishing, and yet all the signal accomplishments of humankind are feats of completion.

Private Choices Eventually Go Public

A great falsehood related to accountability is that your private choices are private. Show me a private choice that does not leak into interpersonal consequences and eventually public ones. It may take time, and we may have to track first-, second-, and third-order consequences, but the effects eventually go public. Gandhi said, "It is wrong and immoral to seek to escape the consequences of one's acts."[5] But can you really escape?

Let's take the example of sexual misconduct. As a teenager I read this statement by historians Will and Ariel Durant and knew it was true: "A youth boiling with hormones will wonder why he should not give full freedom to his sexual desires; and if he is unchecked by custom, morals, or laws, he may ruin his life before he matures sufficiently to understand that sex is a river of fire that must be banked and cooled by a hundred restraints if it is not to consume in chaos both the individual and the group."[6]

Consider one American executive, David Petraeus, who resigned before he was cashiered over allegations and admissions of sexual misconduct.[7] This man was a decorated four-star general and the director of the Central Intelligence Agency, the keeper of the nation's most classified information. This man was sworn to be impenetrable and incorruptible, a human Fort Knox. Yet he forgot that stewardship is moral responsibility for himself, others, and the resources we share. By its very nature, leadership puts pressure on the relationship between stewardship and self-interest. When the two collide, we call it an *ethical dilemma.*

Putting stewardship above self-interest is an act of accountability. Putting self-interest above stewardship is an abdication of accountability. Every leader who has ever committed a moral infraction has to some extent abdicated his role and damaged his contribution as a leader.

The danger is that sexual misconduct can lead to impaired judgment, and impaired judgment can lead to poor decision-making. When a leader misbehaves sexually, he becomes emotionally compromised and less capable of making decisions on behalf of other people. As writer William McGurn observed, "The questions involve less moral judgment than a practical recognition that sexual intimacy is more than a physical act; it leads to emotional entanglements that can take even the most judicious of us to reckless and irresponsible places."[8] Once a leader discards personal accountability in this way, that leader is estranged from humility, which is necessary for balanced and wise judgment.

Of course, not everyone agrees with me. Journalist and author Daniel Gross described a more, shall we say, sophisticated point of view in which virtue is not in fashion. "Evolved people," he claims, "generally accept that marriage is complicated, and that things happen. And so as a general rule, when top professionals admit to, or are caught in, extramarital activity, it is regarded as a sign of human frailty or failing—not as a disqualification or reason to retire."[9] Yes, and would you put your life on the line for a leader after his "evolved" behavior? That's what I thought. It's not just a priggish, puritanical point of view that says infidelity amounts to a lack of accountability. There is simply a much greater risk that the next lapse in judgment will affect you and me. Some people do a pretty good job of compartmentalizing their lives, but eventually private choices go public.

If you exercise poor judgment in your personal life, if you're sexually indiscreet, you become willingly susceptible to the improper influence of another person. Worse yet, what happens if you carry on with that behavior? Chances are you will go until you're caught and then you'll be sorry—and not for your behavior. And if you haven't been caught, you will lack judgment until you *are* caught, like former New York governor Eliot Spitzer, who patronized prostitutes; South Carolina governor Mark Sanford, who would disappear to Argentina on a tryst; or former presidential candidate John Edwards, who had an aide accept the blame for the pregnancy of his campaign worker.

A classic example of such a lack of accountability was Napoleon, who once said, "I have conducted the campaign without consulting anyone. It should have done no good if I had been under the necessity of conforming to the notions of another person."[10]

Avoid a Sense of Entitlement

As a child I watched my grandmother unfold a square of margarine wrapped in tin foil, scrape the foil with a butter knife, and save it in a stack. She would also take the rubber bands off the newspapers and save them in a box. These were the period effects of the Great Depression. Reality tutored her to value things based on scarcity. As a consequence, perhaps, she would infrequently take me for an ice-cream cone after we got the chores done. But that was the exception, which is why I treasured it.

Early in my career, I worked for a company that gave every employee a turkey at Thanksgiving time. It was a cherished, long-standing tradition. One year the economy turned down, and the company decided not to give turkeys. Judging by the sputtering rage that some employees fell into, you would have thought they had been fired without cause. They protested what they saw as an unfair and unilateral decision by management to deprive them of something to which they were justly entitled.

That experience taught me an important leadership principle: the two-turkey rule. One turkey is a gift. Two turkeys are an entitlement. The rule acknowledges the unfortunate reality that that which is given consistently is expected consistently.

The Declaration of Independence says that US citizens have a right to life, liberty, and the pursuit of happiness. Please note that life and liberty are rights, but happiness is not. It's the *pursuit* of happiness that is the right. Happiness is an opportunity, not a guaranteed outcome. The distinction is critical. In many ways entitlement is the opposite of accountability. Instead of feeling answerable for the consequences of your choices, you feel exempt.

There are three different yet related concepts: privileges, entitlements, and rights. According to our common culture, an *entitlement* is more than a privilege and less than a right. It occupies the middle position. You can say that you deserve a turkey based on custom, tradition, or precedent, but you cannot say you have a right to a turkey based on moral principle or natural right. But even that logic won't carry the day. When people want their turkey and there is no turkey to be had, they are not interested in moral reasoning. They simply want the bird. I did not realize that people could become so emotionally attached to frozen poultry and at the same time lose sight of any sense of personal accountability.

In another organization, I witnessed a manager buy lunch for his team two Fridays in a row. The next Friday his workers were lined up outside his door at noon, waiting expectantly for the new benefit. The behavioral conditioning took just two events. As we reward others, we often damage morale in the very act of trying to improve it. We give rewards and then face that mournful day when we have to "take them away." We fail to think through the pain and consequences of dislodging what has become entrenched. So ask yourself the question: *Am I grateful or do I feel entitled to the blessing, privileges, and opportunities of my life?* The answer to that question is a good measure of your personal accountability.

ACCOUNTABILITY: SUMMARY POINTS

Demand accountability of yourself. Hold yourself accountable in the dark.

Check yourself to avoid the three primary forms of deflection:

◆ *Denial*   ◆ *Blame*   ◆ *Excuse*

Remember that hiding is a false concept.

Move from task accountability to project/process accountability and from there to outcome accountability.

Avoid false starts and a regression to the mean by carefully committing to finish what you start.

Put stewardship above self-interest.

Always remember that private choices eventually lead to public consequences.

Recognize the differences among privileges, entitlements, and rights. Resist the temptation to feel entitled.

Chapter 4

The Fourth Cornerstone of Character:

Courage

Whether called to public station or in the more private walks; following no man and no cause because of popularity, shunning no man and no cause you believe to be right because of unpopularity or reproach; but avoiding the parasite and self-seeker, and standing bravely by your own convictions.

Major Simon Willard (1606–1676)
English army major, politician, and magistrate
In a letter to his children

Leadership and the Quantum of Courage

The fourth and final cornerstone of character is courage. The US Marine Corps handbook defines courage in this way: "Moral, mental, and physical strength to resist opposition, face danger, and endure hardship."[1] Does that sound more like leadership or more like management? Leadership requires a larger quantum of courage than management.

It will always be easier to criticize leaders more than managers. Why? Because leaders need more courage to take more risks, which always leads to more unforced errors. Leadership is a tougher game than management. Leaders are burdened with an act of creation. Managers, on the other hand, are burdened with an act of maintenance. Thus, in a strict sense, leaders are creators and managers are caretakers.

Can you be a manager and not a leader? Yes, and every organization needs great managers. Managers run things. But leaders create the things they run. If you lack management skills, you can surround yourself with strong managers and still be successful. Does the principle work in reverse? Can you put a great manager at the helm, surround him or her with great leaders and pull it off? Never. Leaders can compensate for their management deficiencies. Managers cannot compensate for their leadership deficiencies. And courage is at the center of it all.

Author and professor Hugh Nibley observed, "Leaders are movers and shakers, original, inventive, unpredictable, imaginative, full of surprises that discomfit the enemy in war and the main office in peace. For managers are safe, conservative, predictable, conforming organization men [and women] and team players, dedicated to the establishment."[2]

The distinction is overstated, of course. The real world does not allow such a clean division of labor. You have to do both. But the thrust, attitude, and psychology of leadership is different. Leaders create the future. Managers maintain the present. The courage profile is clearly different. Let me illustrate with 20 role differences between the disciplines of leadership and those of management (see figure 4.1).

As disciplines, leadership and management complement and yet compete with each other. They are interdependent but not interchangeable. They represent different roles, but not different people. You cannot claim one and seek dispensation from the other. You must blend them in the right proportions based on need and circumstance. I am not disparaging management but simply pointing out that leadership is a bolder, riskier, more vulnerable role. It simply requires more courage to be a leader.

Think about what leaders do. They are paid to maintain competitive advantage, which by its very nature is perishable. They hold court with the status quo. Managers preserve. Leaders

Figure 4.1 Leadership versus Management Role Differences

LEADERSHIP	MANAGEMENT
Catalyze	Sustain
Create	Duplicate
Tomorrow	Today
Vision	Plans
Strategic	Tactical
Defining goals	Executing goals
Long term	Short term
Possibilities	Facts
Unscripted	Scripted
Disturbing	Preserving
Disequilibrium	Equilibrium
Higher risk	Lower risk
Questions	Answers
People	Things
Hearts	Heads
Influence	Control
Inspiration	Instruction
Meaning	Mechanics
Commitment	Compliance
Context	Content

disturb. Managers follow the script. Leaders write the script. Managers deal with facts. Leaders deal with possibilities. Managers create value today. Leaders create value tomorrow. Managers can run things on the compliance of others. Leaders can only run things on the commitment of others. If not, they cease to lead.

On February 11, 1861, a tall, gangly man in a tailcoat and top hat turned to the townspeople of Springfield, Illinois, before boarding a train that would take him to Washington, DC, where he would assume the presidency of the United States.

With a trembling voice, Abraham Lincoln said,

> Here I have lived a quarter of a century, and have passed from a young to an old man. Here my children have been born, and one is buried. I now leave, not knowing when, or whether ever, I may return, with a task before me greater than that which rested upon Washington. Without the assistance of that Divine Being, who ever attended him, I cannot succeed. With that assistance I cannot fail. Trusting in Him, who can go with me, and remain with you and be every where for good, let us confidently hope that all will yet be well. To His care commending you, as I hope in your prayers you will commend me, I bid you an affectionate farewell.[3]

Lincoln was not leaving to manage the country. He was leaving to lead it. When we sketch the broad contours of leadership against management, we clearly see that courage falls more squarely on the leadership side of the ledger.

The Courage to Keep Trying

When I was a doctoral student at Oxford University, I sat for the oral defense of my dissertation after five years of study. I thought it would be little more than a formality. In fact, my adviser told me to enjoy the experience. "It's ceremonial and perfunctory," he said. I walked out of Nuffield College that day into the dreary

English weather and called my wife, Tracey, in the United States to tell her that I had not passed the exam. That was not part of the plan. I was shattered.

Fortunately, Tracey took the news in stride and told me to get back to work. I regained my courage and determination and passed a year later. My eventual success had little to do with raw intelligence and more to do with courage. I think that's the story most of the time. It's not about taking a moonshot; rather, it's about having the courage to get up and grind it out for one more day, to avoid telling yourself soothing stories that give you a way out.

Stanford psychologist Carol Dweck concluded from her research that "there is *no* relation between students' abilities or intelligence and the development of mastery-oriented qualities. Some of the very brightest students avoid challenges, dislike effort, and wilt in the face of difficulty. And some of the less bright students are real go-getters, thriving on challenge, persisting intensely when things get difficult, and accomplishing more than you expected."[4] Courage is a form of stamina that propels us forward. We become more willing to delay gratification and endure planned deprivation for bigger rewards down the road.

I was in Washington, DC, once and struck up a conversation with a cab driver from Ethiopia. He beamed as he told me he had recently become a US citizen. "This is my country," he said proudly. And then he told me his story. He had come to America eight years earlier with no money, no family, no job, and no education. The only thing he had was some halting English to get around.

Since arriving he had been knocking down barriers. He turned to me and said, "I just earned my college degree." As it turns out, this man had been taking one or two classes per semester at night and driving a cab during the day. He also got married and had a two-year-old son. Here he was, driving one of those beat-up Crown Victoria taxis that should have been donated to the Kidney Foundation, working in the sweltering heat without good air-conditioning, driving around a lot of cranky people day after day—and this guy can't stop smiling and he's telling me America is his country. From this experience, I learned once again that we are all sitting on untapped potential. It takes courage to bring it out. Admiral Hyman G. Rickover said, "Man has a large capacity for effort. In fact it is so much greater than we think it is that few ever reach this capacity."[5]

Whether you are born to privilege or disadvantage, the biggest personal and career limitations reside within you. It always takes courage to reach your potential. Fear means you are scared. Apathy means you don't care. They are two very different things. You can help someone who lacks courage but is willing to put forth effort. Somewhere along the line, my Ethiopian friend got the idea that he could go to college. Too many people still shrink at the prospect of tackling such a big challenge. They haven't had enough personal triumphs to reveal the truth of their own potential. Achieving small wins drip-feeds courage and confidence over time. "Only those who will risk going too far," wrote poet T. S. Eliot, "can possibly find out how far one can go."[6]

The Courage to Listen

It takes courage to listen. It takes even more courage to give people a license to disagree. Great leaders ask people to challenge their ideas, to tell them why something will not work. Consider this statement that Bill Gates made on his final day of work as chairman of Microsoft: "When we miss a big change, when we don't get great people on it, that is the most dangerous thing for us."[7] How do you miss a big change? Microsoft has certainly missed some big ones, including paid search and mobile. Perhaps these experiences have been a formative part of Gates's own development as a leader. Isn't it interesting that current CEO of

Microsoft Satya Nadella said of him, "You can push back on him. He will argue with you vigorously for a couple of minutes, and then he'll be the first person to say, 'Oh, you're right.'"[8]

John Chambers, who served as CEO of Cisco for 20 years, made a similar observation: "My most important decisions are about adjusting to change. Over the last 20 years, we've reinvented ourselves five or six times. Some were positive reinventions, some were very painful. I worry about missing market transitions, shifts in technology, a change in buying patterns. But I think fear is a wasted emotion. You have to change before it becomes obvious."[9] You can cultivate your strategic thinking skills, and you should, but more importantly, you need feedback. You need a tolerance for candor born of humility and courage. It's not only a skill but an ego capacity that you must develop. Otherwise the truth overwhelms us. As poet Emily Dickenson beautifully expressed:

> The truth must dazzle gradually
> Or every man be blind—[10]

General George C. Marshall said of his mentor, General John J. "Black Jack" Pershing, "I have never seen a man who could listen to as much criticism....You could say what you pleased as long as it was straight, constructive criticism."[11] In recent years General Colin Powell, who served as chairman of the Joint Chiefs of Staff, tried to demonstrate the same courageous listening. Whenever he spoke with a low-ranking soldier, Powell said, "I would do everything I could to let him think he was arguing with an equal."[12]

In short, the courage to listen is a competitive advantage whereas not listening is a limiting factor. Writer and professor Jeff Dyer and his colleagues studied Tesla's leadership and culture and concluded, "Learning in an environment of uncertainty requires a willingness to admit mistakes and move quickly rather than digging in and doing nothing for fear of admitting failure. In fact, obsessively attempting to avoid failure can lead to the greater failure of missing the big opportunity."[13]

Why does listening matter so much? It fosters superior performance through the friction of rich dialogue. Disagreement is the natural state of tension that precedes an act of creation or resolution. Can you think of a knotty problem you solved without the need to sift ideas and refine your thinking?

As I work across different industries and social sectors, I see stark differences in patterns of listening. For example, in organizations that rely heavily on hierarchy and rules, the courage to listen and the permission to disagree is typically constrained by a compliant chain of command that is enthroned as the highest organizational principle. A pattern of cautious inquiry and censored disagreement is particularly strong in basic industries, utilities, the military, and law enforcement. Where risk is high and the margin of error is low, paternalism often trumps participation to create a fear-based organization with oceans of silence and undercurrents of rebellion.

Here you find people nodding their heads approvingly, offering gratuitous praise for a proposed course of action, or simply keeping quiet. This pattern indicates compliance out of fear of retribution, artificial consensus out of apathy, and alignment out of lip service. When there's a penalty for disagreement, people stop doing it. And yet it's as natural for people to engage in rigorous debate as it is to rest or play. If you are not allowed to disagree, it's not only undesirable, it's inhuman. When we can't speak our mind, we get the outputs of an echo chamber—unexamined ideas, unscrutinized decisions, and unvetted proposals.

I see a similar pattern in government, education, and healthcare but for different reasons. In these sectors the prevailing culture is to make nice out of a buffered sense of accountability mixed with an elevated sense of purpose. People are generally polite and agreeable, but they listen to be courteous and don't practice penetrating directness when addressing problems and challenges.

Finally, there's the technology sector—whose very survival is based on innovation. The cultural DNA of most technology firms is one of robust dialogue and hard-hitting debate. Leaders in this space don't always open the door to passion and insight and close it on rancor, strife, and contention, but they are the best I've seen. Part of what the successful tech firms of the world are proving is that the real incubator of innovation is the social production system—the way people interact and solve problems. If you can really listen to people and tolerate and channel disagreement, you have found a source of competitive advantage.

There is a right way to render a contrary opinion. It's the leader's job to listen without being defensive or disagreeable. The way an *organization* handles disagreement is a primary measure of culture and an accurate predictor of performance. The way an *individual* handles disagreement is a primary measure of emotional intelligence and an accurate predictor of leadership potential. Do you disagree?

The Courage to Customize Your Candor

I have labored the point that leaders have a duty to be honest and straightforward. They should not disguise the truth or mislead people by making things appear better or different than they really are. For example, when Antarctic explorer Earnest Shackleton put an advertisement in a London newspaper in 1913, he was candid about what his recruits would likely encounter on the ocean voyage. There was no trace of false advertising, no bait and switch, no silk waistcoat on the hog: "Men wanted for hazardous journey. Small wages, bitter cold. Long months of complete darkness. Constant danger. Safe return doubtful. Honour and recognition in case of success."[14]

The next step is to customize the candor based on context and need. What if we are talking about personal feedback? Is candor still the right thing? Is it an absolute? In leadership development, we often talk about the quality of being coachable. A highly coachable person is someone who receives feedback well. The more coachable a person is, the more capacity that person has to accept the truth of his or her own behavior and performance and make improvements.

The ability to receive candid feedback is largely a measure of character. It would be nice if we could all withstand a full and unsparing reflection of ourselves, but we can't. Actually, I should qualify that. We can but won't. We are unwilling. We reject the feedback we're not willing to act on. We cover our ears and sing to block out inconvenient truths. We engage in denial to avoid a state of cognitive dissonance. For example, Thomas Jefferson was perpetually unable to live within his means and died with enormous debt which he bequeathed to his posterity. He refused to confront the reality of his own behavior and circumstances.[15]

In my experience it's only a small fraction of the population that can consistently withstand full self-disclosure. So, any candor given beyond a person's ability to receive it is wasted and may be destructive. It's like putting a steak in front of a toddler—it's not consumable. Here is the principle: Leaders must weigh the consequences of candor to best serve the person and the organization. That is not easy, especially when a person is performing poorly and lacks self-awareness.

I know a leader who likes to remind people that he is blunt. He advertises this quality as a sign of courage. He takes pride in the fact that he treats everyone with unmitigated candor, as if to imply that most people are too political and self-serving and can't approach his level of dispassionate judgment. In reality, this man is not demonstrating courage. He is carelessly spewing whatever is on his mind. He is selfish, oblivious, and showing poor judgment in the feedback he gives. He is the one who needs a full dose of candor, to comprehend that some people can handle it only in small doses. He is plagued by an inflated self-appraisal.

The question is this: *How much candor is a person willing to receive?* That is a judgment call. If you are paying attention, you can usually tell when people reach their limit, as if they have eaten a hearty meal and can't take another bite. At the point of satiation, people show signs of stress overload and defensiveness. Candor is no longer useful because it's no longer actionable. More is worse. Further, candor given without care and compassion is painful, sometimes brutal, and serves no purpose.

As parents, we see this with our children. As coaches, we see this with our players. As managers in organizations, we see this with our employees. As husbands and wives, we see this with our spouses. We always hope the capacity to receive honest feedback will increase. In the end, each person decides how far to open the door and how much reality to let in. Those with moral strength swing wide the door. Those who lack it slam and double-bolt the door. Sometimes we have to force open the door with tough love. But even then it's a choice to receive the candor. We need to remember that.

Finally, avoid personal attacks. First, it is always wrong to embarrass, demean, or belittle someone. Second, personal attacks are instruments of either coercion or manipulation that evoke defensiveness, which makes it even less likely that a person will receive feedback. Instead, use the more potent method of building and encouraging those you are trying to coach: you cannot lead people effectively if you don't love them.

The Courage to Avoid Profanity

It may seem strange to address profanity here, but I have discovered that it's a reliable measure of courage. One of the biggest obstacles to finding your voice is simply having the courage to leave the sheepfold. And one of the areas in which I see lem-minglike conformity and an alarming lack of courage is in the poor language many people use. Most are content to follow the dictates of fashion and cave to the relentless spamming of the human mind, to choose trash over treasure.

I grew up in locker rooms and spent several years in heavy manufacturing, and because humans can't close their ears the way they can their lips, I heard more profanity than a gangsta lyricist can stuff into a rap ballad.

Our popular culture drips with profanity. In business and politics, profanity has a long and distinguished past, as well. But I mean distinguished in the G. K. Chesterton sense of the word, as when he said, "The vulgar man is always the most distinguished, for the very desire to be distinguished is vulgar."[16]

Consider the meaning of the term *profanity*. It comes from Latin roots that mean "before or outside the temple," referring to language that is irreverent or indecent. In modern usage, *profanity* refers to language that is vulgar, crude, profligate, or immoral. Effusions of profanity have always echoed through the halls of power. But why?

Members of the refined and genteel class are said to use profanity sparingly and for effect, as garlic in the salad of taste. As English essayist Jonathan Swift once said, "A footman may swear, but he cannot swear like a lord. He can swear as often, but can he swear with equal delicacy, propriety, and judgment?"[17] Apparently, there's a proper and sophisticated way to be profane.

Teens sprinkle their language with scatological references to gain social acceptance. Sometimes they do it out of rebellion. I'm somewhat sympathetic because adults are the ones who teach them that it's adult to talk that way, though it has nothing to do with maturity.

Soldiers swear exuberantly as an extension of teenage bravado. Unfortunately, profanity is a cowardly custom of military culture that represents the lowest possible barrier to entry into a fraternity that is supposed to be defined by bravery. That is a contradiction. If you lace your language with expletives, you can join this elite club.

Shock jocks use profanity as the weapon of the witless because they have no real talent, but that matters little to a market that has no real taste. I listened to a famous shock jock once for about two minutes, and that was two minutes too long. Without the profanity he was dead air. Writers attempt to use it judiciously, to be endearing, authentic, and down-to-earth.

How about corporate executives? Many of them use profanity as a menacing display of alpha behavior. It's a way to express dominance, claim territory, and warn would-be challengers.

Finally, profanity can be an emotional relief valve in moments of pain. As Mark Twain, one of our greatest humorists, put it, "There ought to be a room in every house to swear in. It's dangerous to have to repress an emotion like that."[18] We don't like to admit it, but profanity is vanity. In most cases, using it is an indulgence. It's a form of arrogant satisfaction. It's exhibitionism but not in any distinctive sense. These days it's about as original as getting a tattoo. In other words, it's an act of conformity, not an act of courage.

I invite you to take courage, rebel against popular culture, and find your own voice. I dare you to have something to say and to find strong and powerful words with which to say it. The English language is beautiful, flexible, and inexhaustible. I invite you to drop the sleazy slang and communicate more clearly and honestly. Listen to Shakespeare's Henry V hold forth in his St. Crispin's Day speech. That will shake the glazing out of your windows.

The Courage to Aim High

My teenage daughter once completed a weeklong volleyball camp. Every night she came home exhausted and exhilarated. She set goals for conditioning, serving, bumping, blocking, and diving. The days were long, intense, and highly structured. In this case, a good system combined with great coaches accelerated her development in just a few days.

My other teenage daughter spent the week working at an assisted-living center. It's not a glamorous job. She helps prepare the meals, feed the elderly residents, and clean up. She is getting to know the residents by name and is learning about their needs and preferences. One woman insists on a straw with her drink. Another needs to be spoon-fed. There is no limelight shining on my daughter in the care center. There are no whistles, no cheering, and no high-fives. But guess what? She comes home with the same sweet exhaustion and exhilaration, the same sense of earned accomplishment.

When I see one of my children wearing a tired smile, I smile. Good things are happening. The same is true for all of us. When we set and achieve meaningful goals, we stretch, build capacity, gain confidence, and learn what it means to contribute. When we find success, we want to do it again and we are inclined to fill our bucket list with meaningful goals.

When people don't taste real success, they often go looking elsewhere for fulfillment. They may get the idea that pleasurable pursuits are the equivalent of earned achievement. That is of course what our popular culture teaches, and people tend to believe what they are taught. The truth is that much of the pleasure we seek offers no reward. It leads to mediocrity, untapped potential, and even destructive addictions.

Think about children. They need experiences that will help them believe in themselves. If children pass through childhood and have amassed nothing but hours on the gaming, Internet, and television log, it is a lost childhood. Now think about adults. It's exactly the same: if you pass the years in the pursuit of pleasure, power, and prestige, you lay waste to your adulthood. Remember, goals fire the imagination. They are powerful because they contain both intellectual and emotional pull.

How do you set meaningful goals? Here are some guidelines:

- Easy is not exciting. Don't aim too low.

- Motivate but don't disable. The higher the goal, the higher the chance of failure, so don't aim too high.

- Start with small, visible, measurable goals. Small successes are enormously powerful in building confidence. Now string them together.

- Your goal depends on your starting point and where you have been. If you have a string of failures behind you, or you simply want to break out of your inertia, you need a small success to get some confidence and momentum back.

- Generate excitement, anticipation, and a little pressure.

- Understand that the grand aim in life is not to consume but to create and contribute. It's a whole lot more fulfilling.

- Identify projects to complete, service to render, and skills to develop.

My youngest son came to me recently with a look of sheer delight. He proudly announced that he had read Roald Dahl's *Matilda* in one day. And then he proceeded to tell me all about it. You can't put a price on that.

Ah, but a man's reach should exceed his grasp,
Or what's a heaven for?[19]

So wrote poet Robert Browning. It takes courage to reach above the kitsch and idleness that increasingly dominate our popular culture. When we do, we are leading.

COURAGE: SUMMARY POINTS

Leaders are responsible to create; managers are responsible to curate.

Have the courage to disturb the status quo when it needs to be disturbed.

Recognize that in the long run success has more to do with courage than it does raw intelligence.

Develop quiet courage and avoid the soft quit through the discipline of consistent daily performance.

The courage to listen is a competitive advantage, whereas the arrogance to not listen is a limiting factor.

Give people a license to disagree. Eliminate penalties for disagreement, except for personal attacks.

Customize your candor based on the capacity of the person to receive and act on it.

Have the courage to rebel against our popular culture's indulgence in profanity and vulgarity.

Find your unique, independent voice to say strong and meaningful things.

Set stretch goals that motivate and fire your imagination; avoid unrealistic goals that demoralize and disable.

PART TWO

The Four Cornerstones of Competence

I F CHARACTER IS THE INFRASTRUCTURE, COMPETENCE IS THE superstructure. Competence is about skill, adeptness, and mastery. It's the quality or state of being able to do things and of doing them well. There are of course many areas of technical competence or specialized expertise, but I'm referring to the attributes that lead to general and sustainable competence as a leader.

Learning

The first cornerstone of competence is learning. The *learning* imperative in the twenty-first century is to learn at or above the speed of change. Thus, the learning disposition of a leader in this context must be agile, aggressive, self-directed, and collaborative. Many people are still deeply socialized with an industrial age learning mind-set based on dependency and learned helplessness under the tutelage of benevolent organizations. Leaders today must reject that model as they constantly identify and close their own learning gaps.

Change

The second cornerstone of competence is change. *Change* has always been a constant, but in today's accelerating environment there's a greater compression of time frames. Leaders must assume the continuous loss of competitive advantage and build resilience to confront one adaptive challenge after another. This is an intellectual and emotional capacity. It means that you act preemptively when you can. It means you avoid muscling or smuggling change with others. It means you change culture by design rather than by default.

Judgment

The third cornerstone of competence is judgment. *Judgment* allows you to see the big picture and think through the intended and unintended consequences of different courses of action. Judgment helps you select the right people and customize the development needs of each individual. With judgment you are able to discern the motivations and abilities of others and delegate properly. Judgment helps you know whom to listen to. Finally, judgment helps you learn from success and failure, avoid discouragement and contentment, and maintain appropriate urgency.

Vision

The fourth cornerstone of competence is vision. *Vision* is to see what does not exist. It's a portrait of the future and a seedling of reality. Modest plans do not stir your blood. They don't get you on your feet and put you in motion. Vision does. We draw strength from vision when circumstances conspire against us. We draw creativity from vision because it unshackles us from convention and orthodoxy. And we draw vision itself from a sense of our own identity. While information merely informs, vision inspires.

CHAPTER 5

The First Cornerstone
of Competence:
Learning

*In a time of drastic change it is the learners who
inherit the future. The learned usually find themselves
equipped to live in a world that no longer exists.*

Eric Hoffer (1902–1983)
Author and moral and social philosopher
Reflections on the Human Condition (1973)

The Most Important Thing You Can Learn

The first cornerstone of competence is learning. On one occasion
I had the opportunity to advise leaders at a technology company.
On one visit to the company, I struck up a conversation with
a gentleman and learned that he trained people in cell phone
forensics. I asked him how often he had to update his teaching
curriculum to stay current with technology. Answer: every two
months. Can you imagine your knowledge and skills becoming
obsolete in eight weeks? This may be the exception, but it
illustrates the hyperspeed of change in the twenty-first century.

The question is, *What are you going to do about it?* The new
normal is visible to all but not felt by all. Are you still untouched
and unconverted by the riptide of change? You may not feel
it now, but eventually we must all yield or bow out. The new
normal antagonizes the inflexible, persecutes the nonlearner, and

punishes the resister. The placid years of docile domestic markets are gone. The cherished employer/employee compact is gone. The "learn, earn, and burn" model of career progression—learn your profession, earn your living, and burn your banked resources during your golden years—that's gone too.

The compression of time frames and the scope of global integration have created a universal imperative: learn at or above the speed of change. Many baby boomers have obsolescent skills and an outdated learning mind-set. They are hanging on by emotionally cocooning themselves, trying to avoid career misfortune until retirement, enduring on the basis of skills from another time, immobilized, publically acknowledging the new world but privately unwilling to learn in it.

The Gen Xers and millennials have a different version of the same problem. They are often passive because they have been sedated by technology. They have superficial agility to run apps and move around the Internet, but they often lack the hard-core problem-solving skills and discipline to see a conflict through to resolution. Yes, they are digital natives, but learning is more than navigating technology. It's about aggressive self-directedness, tenacity, and sustained concentration.

Here is the principle: The single most important thing you can learn in school is how to learn when you get out of school.[1] Why? Because once you leave school and its structured environment, for the rest of your life your learning will overwhelmingly be based on your ability to learn on your own—without a teacher, a classroom, or a curriculum. It will be informal learning, and it will be up to you to retool, rescript, and recalibrate yourself.

The good news is that you have a motivational advantage when you direct your own learning. As academic Ken Bain discovered, "People learn most effectively when they are trying to answer their own questions."[2] Horace Greeley said of Lincoln, he "gladly profited by the teaching of events and circumstances, no matter how adverse or unwelcome....There was probably no year of his life that he was not a wiser, cooler, better man than he had been the year preceding."[3] That is the model.

People learn differently. Some people don't like academic work and the didactic approach. They are purpose-driven learners and flourish in a hands-on work environment because there's a real and immediate application of what they are learning.[4] Ultimately, *how* we learn matters less than *that* we learn. You may learn through dialogue, data, stories, visual images, or trial and error.

Unfortunately, most of our schools don't teach students to learn on their own. Instead they breed dependency to an industrial welfare model of learning. Through the generations many people have been socialized to rely on the machinery of an institution to carry them along. That doesn't work anymore. Many organizations have adjusted to a self-directed model, but many others are disoriented and frightened by the idea of learning, unlearning, and relearning. They are fighting reality and the threat of encroaching obsolescence at the same time. They will lose both fights.

Have you ever been totally prepared for a new job, assignment, project, or promotion? Me neither. With every new assignment, there is some kind of knowledge or skills gap. Sometimes the organization will help you close the gap but never all the way. In the end you have to own the gap and figure out how to close it yourself. If you don't, your value depreciates over time.

There are few principles in organizational life that have died such a violent and ignominious death as the idea of permanent competence. Despite the fact that many of us stubbornly cling to the old thinking, it is stunningly clear that much of our knowledge and many of our skills have become temporary assets. Randy McDonald, the vice president of human resources (HR) at IBM, once said that 22 percent of IBM's total employee population would have obsolete skills in three years.[5] We simply have never before encountered the speed and complexity that we see in the current environment. And that's on top of our own natural tendency to become rigid.

We get deeply grooved, and if we stay in the grooves, our performance suffers. We get the same results while others around us improve theirs. There is always natural decay and inertia. The question is, *Will we recognize and respond to it?*

For centuries society embraced a *permanent learning* model: learning once for permanent qualification. In other words, you could acquire a skill that would last for the duration of your work life. For example, my grandfather was a conductor for the Union Pacific railroad. He learned how to operate a locomotive, and that skill remained relevant throughout his career. He never experienced an obsolescence cycle and never had to retool.

With time that learning model was replaced with *continuous learning:* continuous learning for ongoing qualification.

Finally, we are now in the midst of another transition to *agile learning:* rapid, collaborative, and self-directed learning at the moment of need. In other words, learning at or above the speed of change requires that we learn together through a social process, work through rapid cycles of learning and testing, and do it on demand (see figure 5.1).[6]

Today leaders are called on to model the patterns of agile learning. This requires a very different emotional and social posture that can feel personally threatening to one's confidence. Howard Schultz, CEO of Starbucks, said in an interview, "The hardest thing about being a leader is demonstrating or showing vulnerability."[7] Leaders must become comfortable portraying themselves as competent through their ability to learn and adapt, rather than on the basis of their current knowledge and skills, let alone their title, position, and authority.

Figure 5.1 The Evolution of Learning

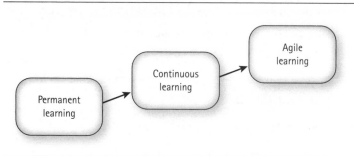

Clearly, learning agility is different from competence. Competence means you have the knowledge and skills you need to create value today. Learning agility, on the other hand, is the ability to continuously acquire new knowledge and skills during and ahead of changes in the market. You may be highly competent, but competence today is not necessarily a good predictor of competence tomorrow. Learning agility is. It provides the best-known gauge of future competitiveness. Some of the most competent leaders this week will stumble and fail next week precisely because they are not learning at or above the speed of change.

Leaders must build confidence in themselves and others through cycles of learning and unlearning. They must accept the fact that they will pass through periods of temporary incompetence, and sometimes even failure, as they move through inflection points in their careers. But they will do so based on their underlying ability and willingness to learn. What is different today is that credibility is based on personifying the qualities of an agile learner more than those of an expert.

Here are some questions to help you assess your own personal learning disposition:

- Do you see knowledge and skills as perishable?

- Do you believe that learning is where advantage comes from, that it represents the highest form of enterprise risk management, and that the biggest risk an individual or organization can take is to cease to learn?

- Do you possess deep patterns of aggressive and self-directed learning?

- Do you lead by the way you learn?

The Risk of Standing Still

In 1950, the inaugural season of Formula One auto racing, the average tire-changing pit stop took about 60 seconds. Today this choreographed dance takes less than three seconds. The question is not *Are you knowledgeable and skillful?* The question is *Will you stay knowledgeable and skillful as the ground shifts under your feet?*

The ability to be valuable to an organization through agile learning becomes more important as the organization struggles to compete. Let's say your boss announces that your company is restructuring the department, acquiring a competitor, outsourcing a function, or entering a new market. What goes through your head? *I could lose my job, my compensation, my influence, my expertise, my credibility, my seniority, my office, my friends, my, my, my...*

That gripping fear is not irrational. Human beings are for the most part savvy risk managers who buck and bristle at the prospect of change. Yet the natural instinct to recoil can be dangerously wrong, especially when it comes to learning. You cannot run away from it. As they say at the US Marine Corps sniper school, "You can run, but you'll just die tired."

Show me a company that has stood still in its market over the past two years while reaping handsome profits. My point is a simple one: If organizations need to move with greater agility to sustain competitive advantage, what does that mean for you?

You have to move with the caravan or risk irrelevance. Competitive advantage is not just an organizational concept; it's also an individual one.

Think about it this way: There are really only two paths to competitive advantage—low cost or high value. If you can deliver both, that's a breakthrough. Firms win when they become low-cost producers or provide high value through some kind of distinctiveness. The same logic applies to human beings. Either you provide high value by delivering distinct quality or you become commoditized, in which case the market gets you on the cheap. Ultimately, as author Thomas A. Stewart argues, "Wealth is the product of knowledge."[8] It's Darwinian and harsh in a sense, but it's very real: there's a supply/demand function with your name on it, and the market will pay you what it thinks you're worth.

In a prior life, I had the opportunity to sit at the table in union negotiations to hammer out collective-bargaining agreements. I learned about a concept called *job security*. The idea was that an organization could promise this to an employee. When you talk to millennials about job security, they cannot comprehend it. It's science fiction to them. The standstill career has always been the path of least resistance. Now it's the path of ultimate risk. The following practical questions will help you avoid the risks of standing still.

Do you own your career? Do you take complete ownership of your career development? Sure, your organization may have systems in place to help you. There may be training, coaching, action learning, and the annual review. That is fine. Accept the help. But it makes no sense to entrust the planning and fate of your career to an organization whose fortunes will ride on the volatile waves of unpredictable markets.

Do you view your skills as technology? Professional skills today are more like technology. They go through a similar product life cycle of introduction, growth, maturity, and decline. Do you have the mind-set that you must abandon skills as they become obsolete and requalify yourself with new ones?

Are you an agile learner? Organizations normally provide training and tools to help employees achieve competency, but there will always be knowledge and skill gaps that you alone must close. Independent learners close those gaps based on their own assessment and self-directed learning strategies.[9] Dependent learners wait around for the organization to do it for them. Never place a bet on the organization to deliver you. Charles Eliot, the president of Harvard at the turn of the twentieth century, said we all need "the trained capacity for mental labor, rapid, intense, and sustained."[10]

Do you view the organization as configurable parts? For many people, the "reorg" is an emotionally disturbing experience. Is this true for you? There's nothing sacred about processes, systems, structure, roles, and responsibilities; they are simply components we use to organize and perform work in the service of a business strategy. Agile, high-performing employees understand this. They view organizations as dynamic systems with configurable parts, so don't get emotionally attached. Focus on creating value. If the organization is performing well, terrific. If it is not, it's time to dine at a new table.

Do you find fulfillment in learning? Learning is vital to your competitiveness and contribution, but don't forget that it carries its own reward. It brings inherent satisfaction. Philosopher and political economist John Stuart Mill said,

> Next to selfishness, the principal cause which makes life unsatisfactory is want of mental cultivation. A cultivated

mind—I do not mean that of a philosopher, but any mind to which the fountains of knowledge have been opened, and which has been taught, in any tolerable degree, to exercise its faculties—finds sources of inexhaustible interest in all that surrounds it; in the objects of nature, the achievements of art, the imaginations of poetry, the incidents of history, the ways of mankind, past and present, and their prospects in the future.[11]

Don't Bet on the Organization

I distinctly remember a conversation I once had with an employee. He said his father told him, "If you can get on at [XYZ Company], you're set for life." He was telling his son to pin his star to the company. That advice reminds me of a children's book I used to read to my kids, *Are You My Mother?* by P. D. Eastman. It's an endearing story. The problem is that some people look to their employers in this way. Many people still have the maternal paradigm. It's not prudent career advice. *If only I can get on at such and such tech company, I'll be set* goes this hypothesis of career management. If you can get on, that's fantastic, but don't mistakenly believe that the organization is your mother and the source of your job security.

Such a belief is dangerously misguided in the twenty-first century. The world today is most unaccommodating of such a strategy. The impermanence of things makes it so. We may yearn for stability and something to hold on to, but we must stop using the concept of job security and replace it with the concept of personal competitiveness. The source of your competitive advantage is you.

Writer V. S. Naipaul, who won the Nobel Prize for literature, once reflected on his upbringing in Trinidad with these words: "Small places with simple economies bred small people with simple destinies."[12] And so it was. But can it still be? Can we choose to live that way? Is there really a choice to compete in a small, simple economy?

The central drama of our economy is accelerating change, which translates into demand for well-prepared human capital. Yet we witness the thinning and hollowing out of the middle class in the United States. Why is it thinning? The answer is simple: large swaths of the middle class are not prepared to meet the new demands of the labor market. I spend much of my time with tech companies in Silicon Valley. I can tell you they all compete on a global standard of competitiveness and would never consider hiring mediocre talent.

I talk to a lot of people these days who flit from job to job. It's a lot like the mail-order workout programs that promote the concept of muscle confusion. Exercising based on muscle confusion is better than not exercising at all. Cross-training can be very effective, but the concept that maximum results come from constantly changing your workout routine to keep your muscles guessing is only partially correct. Changing your routine can be helpful to avoid burnout, but to achieve maximum performance you must continue to increase both the volume (repetitions) and the load (weight).

In the end, maximum performance comes from high and sustained focus on the same activity but with increasing levels of difficulty. If you frequently change the activity, you will actually plateau your performance after a short time, and you'll be mediocre at everything and outstanding at nothing. Agility is important, but if you shift too much, performance suffers. It's like trying to increase productivity with more multitasking.

Learn Your Living

Is it better to say that we learn our living instead of earn it? Strangely, to be credentialed implies that the process of learning is complete. It suggests that you are somehow permanently qualified, that you can sit back and enjoy being smart. Of course that's ridiculous, but what percentage of college graduates do you think are bona fide agile learners? Many are on education welfare. They read a book a year. Sometimes it's the formal education itself that gets in the way of learning. Albert Einstein observed, "It is, in fact, nothing short of a miracle that the modern methods of instruction have not yet entirely strangled the holy curiosity of inquiry."[13] But that can be an excuse, too.

One thing is certainly clear: the future belongs to learners. Think about the mercurial world in which we live and the protean organizations in which we work. Who will lead in the days and years ahead? The answer is affirmatively those who have a demonstrated ability for agile learning. They may not be the most credentialed among us, especially as education continues to democratize and credentials become diluted.

The connection between learning and leadership is unmistakable. It used to be that for most every problem you encountered, there was someone close by who had seen it before. Not so anymore. Many of the challenges we now face have no precedent. There is no institutional memory to come to our aid. We simply have to acknowledge the individual as the source of productive capacity based on learning—but it is the leader who must set the example and model the way.

You Were Born Curious

Watch toddlers. They meet each day with a sense of wonder. But with many of us, something happened on the way to adulthood: our curiosity flamed out.

A nation whose citizens binge on television, the mass media, and the Internet would not appear to be a highly curious nation. Rather, we seem to be suffering from an epidemic failure of imagination. As a society, we rely on the curious. It's not out-landish to say that jobs are traceable to curious people and that our economy relies on them. They are the ones who puzzle until their puzzlers are sore.

You don't read about curious people in economics textbooks or policy circles, yet they are the real job creators. It's the curious who ask the brave questions and solve the wicked problems. They create new value, new industries, and new opportunities. They are the ones who bring fresh perspective to overcome the grooved thinking and calcified bias that chain us to the status quo. All hail the curious among us who invent and innovate and propel us forward.

During the Great Recession, we accumulated a deficit of several million jobs. The permafunk lifted, but job creation is not what it needs to be. We need more curious people solving more problems to create more jobs. How? By encouraging them. By finding out what motivates them. By praising effort more than results. By letting them test and learn. By letting them fail fast and forward. By giving them problems that need solutions. By eliminating bureaucracy and disincentives that get in their way. By getting rid of staid educational methods that constrain rather than unleash fresh thinking.

Referring to our educational system, Bill Gates said, "People who are as curious as I am will be fine in any system. For the self-motivated student, these are the golden days. I wish I was growing up now. I envy my son. If he and I are talking about something that we don't understand, we just watch videos and click on articles, and that feeds our discussion. Unfortunately, the highly curious student is a small percentage of the kids."[14]

Gates is an off-the-charts curious person. There are many people who are curious but don't know it because society has stifled their curiosity. Many young people pass their discretionary time glued to technology yet not learning. They have not been curious for years, and they hardly notice. What they need is someone to take a personal interest in them and help them rekindle their curiosity.

It's important to understand that curiosity is more about motivation than smarts. Sir John Gurdon, a developmental biologist at Oxford and winner of the Nobel Prize, ranked last in biology out of the 250 boys in his class at Eton. On his report card, the teacher said it would be a sheer waste of time for him to study science. He took that advice and studied literature in college. But in his graduate work, he rejected the advice and switched back to science because he was curious.[15]

What are you interested in? is a question that can lead to a vein of motivation in a young mind. When a teacher, parent, or employer mines a vein of motivation in someone, that person accelerates, develops confidence, and increases capacity. When you find motivation in a problem, the problem becomes what Sir John Gurdon calls "a problem of interest." In other words, it becomes a problem you want to tackle and solve. We need more curious people chasing more problems of interest.

Ask More Questions

There is a principle in leadership that says the further you advance in responsibility, the more you must rely on questions rather than answers to do your job well. The exception to the rule might be working at a fast-food restaurant, if you have done every job on the floor by the time you're promoted to management. You can flip the burgers, deep-fry the fries, ring the register, mop the floor, and reconcile the inventory of napkins and ketchup.

Most organizations, however, are far too complex for anyone to master the enterprise. You cannot possibly move through all the chairs. And even if you did, the pace of change would overtake you. Why, then, do so many leaders frantically try to maintain their status as a curator and clearinghouse of solutions? Why do so many think that the essence of leadership is about directing and dispatching people? I suggest that these leaders ask themselves what year it is. I was talking to the CEO of a hospital not long ago. He said to me, "I have 10 direct reports on my team. Do you know how many of their jobs I can do?"

"How many?" I asked.

"None," he stated emphatically. "I can't do a single one. And if you go down a level to their direct reports, it's the same story."

Can this hospital CEO possibly lead with answers? Absurd. His job is to know the right questions to ask. Questioning skills will make or break him. If you have been deeply socialized to understand that your job as a leader is primarily about telling people what to do, you may have some unlearning to do. Failing to do so could become a career derailer and even a fatal flaw if you don't replace the old behavior.

The Test of Obviousness

In working with groups of leaders, I often facilitate a three-level questioning exercise in which I ask them to take a current challenge in the organization and come up with questions about it. I divide the leaders into groups of five and ask them to identify 10 questions about the issue. They often say they have already studied the issue from every possible angle. I smile and ask them to humor me. That is level one—the *test of obviousness*. It's playing journalist and asking the *who, what, when, where,* and *why.* The first 10 questions are not so hard. Then I quote Winston Churchill, "Now this is not the end. It is not even the beginning of the end. But it is, perhaps, the end of the beginning."[16] I explain that in level one we normally pass the test of obviousness by observing and considering basic cause-and-effect relationships.

The Test of Obscurity

In round two I ask the leaders to come up with 10 more questions about the issue at hand. It takes more mental muscle, but it's only when we push harder that we start to uncover new options and possibilities. We grow our powers of observation and analysis. That is level two—the *test of obscurity*—digging deeper to see what isn't obvious. The magic begins when we start to discard convention, throw off shackled thinking, and abandon orthodoxy. The line between naïveté and brilliance can be very thin. Remember the old adage: there are no stupid questions.

The Test of Originality

Finally, we do a third round with 10 more questions to push the limits. In the third round—the *test of originality*—leaders feel the pain. They bump up against the boundaries of their intellectual agility. But it's here that we see them come up with the most beautiful questions. As we move from round to round, leaders normally discover the following four important principles.

Questions lead to questions. In other words, new questions are found inside old questions.

Questions naturally progress from general to specific. Our mental processes tend to follow an inverted pyramid in which we ask general and basic questions first and then graduate to narrow and penetrating ones later.

Questions tend to shift from an internal to an external perspective. We tend to be self-centered and ethnocentric about the questions we ask at first. Gradually, we get outside of ourselves and ask questions from different vantage points.

The best questions come last and are hard-won. It's where the treasure of original thinking, creativity, and innovation is found.

Learning More Effectively

Why did Yo-Yo Ma, Itzhak Perlman, and Vladimir Horowitz become virtuoso musicians when others who practiced just as hard and just as long did not? World-class performers clearly learn faster. Can the rest of us learn faster, too? It's fair to say we have not reached terminal learning velocity in any field. How much faster can we learn? I am convinced that increasing learning speed is one of the great frontiers of our time. For many reasons we need to bring people to competency, if not mastery, more quickly.

One day I was in the gym rebounding balls for my 14-year-old son. As I stood below the basket, dishing the ball back to him, I asked him who the best three-point shooter in the NBA was. He said Steph Curry. I asked him how long it would take to be able to shoot like Steph Curry. Would it take 10,000 hours?—which is roughly equivalent to 15 years of year-round basketball practice and game time. My son's response was telling: "I don't see why it needs to take that long."

A group of psychologists—including most notably the late Benjamin Bloom and more recently K. Anders Ericsson—have done empirical studies to figure out what it takes to achieve mastery in a particular field. The results are fairly consistent. It takes 10,000 hours of practice to achieve world-class performance in almost any field of endeavor. Can we break the so-called 10,000-hour rule? Ericsson tells us that not only do we need the 10,000 hours but we also need to engage in *deliberate practice,* which he defines as "considerable, specific, and sustained efforts to do something you *can't* do well."[17] So, genius is a combination of natural endowment, outside support, and deliberate practice. But can we make our deliberate practice even better and cut into that 10,000-hour requirement? Can we become even quicker studies?

There are several concepts that relate to deliberate practice, such as flow state, meta-cognition, executive function, effective effort, and high engagement. All of these refer more or less to the supervisory attention or cognitive control system of a human being. Researchers found that if a person can stay focused by regulating impulses, that person learns faster. In other words, if you can develop the discipline to avoid distractions, you can assimilate information and develop skills more quickly.

What orthodoxies must we discard to come to competency faster? First, the dominant culture of teaching and coaching in our society is often too directive. There's too much telling and advocacy and not enough questioning and aided discovery. How often is the coach or teacher the limiting factor?

When I played college football, it was all about getting the "reps," and there was little if any effort made to help players understand how to coach themselves. Today the directive teaching model is bumping up against its inherent limits. In the workplace, for instance, employees must be able to innovate their own performance, disrupt themselves, conduct their own assessments and interventions, conduct careful postmortems of performance, and reflect methodically on what went well and not so well.

As author and speaker Geoff Colvin observes, they must be able "to spot nonobvious information that's important."[18] Translation: Give more *what* and *why* and less *how* to those you serve. The more you direct, the less they do. The less you direct, the more they have to figure it out. This encourages stretch and builds analytic skills and generative capacity. Focus on creating more-tenacious learners, with more intellectual and emotional self-reliance and higher powers of concentration.

The New Learning Imperative

The learning tradition of our society has for centuries been based on two enduring patterns. First is *informal learning,* or on-the-job training. Throughout history it was customary to apprentice young workers in the skilled trades by having them observe and work alongside master craftsmen until they acquired enough knowledge and skill to work independently. The second pattern is *formal learning,* in which a mentor teaches students through formal instruction. This pattern traces its origin to the empires of antiquity and later to the centers of learning established by religious orders.

For centuries society held to these two approaches—one experiential, the other didactic. These two traditions have lasted this long because of society's division of labor: we need the experiential approach to train for applied skills and the didactic approach to train knowledge workers in the generation and evaluation of ideas. That distinction is now blurred, as stable markets and incremental change are less the norm. Now we witness wave after wave of market disruption. As markets become more dynamic, we are internalizing at a deeper level the fact that people are the true source of competitive advantage.

Even hard-core authoritarian bosses, conditioned in another time and place, can now be found yielding to the new reality, seeking counsel, and soliciting input from their people. Most of the time the tools change before the culture does. We have learning technologies such as wikis, blogs, social networks, open-source, open-content, file-sharing, peer production, virtual communities, microlearning, and many kinds of performance support tools. Organizations are still very much in transition with a lot of work to do before the new learning mind-set descends fully into the cultural soil.

In fact, most organizations still tolerate a significant amount of nonlearning from employees. They toss around learning mantras, slogans, and expectations, but agile learning is not ingrained in people and there's no real accountability for new learning behavior. To some extent the age of mass collaboration has brought with it the assumption that everyone is prepared and willing to participate in peer production and co-creation activities. Collectively, we are not there. Technology has lowered the cost of learning and collaboration.[19] It's our behavior that lags behind. But individually, you can get there as fast as you want. The problem is more motivation than access.

LEARNING: SUMMARY POINTS

Preemptively assess your personal competitive advantage and identify your learning gaps before the organization does.

Triage your learning gaps and develop an informal curriculum to close them.

Demonstrate the aggressive, self-directed habits of an agile learner.

Plan to abandon your current skills as they become obsolete.

Spend less time watching TV, gaming, and surfing the Internet.

Rekindle your curiosity by reevaluating your interests and motivations.

Relentlessly ask penetrating questions that move through the tests of obviousness, obscurity, and originality.

Remember that the line between naïveté and brilliance can be very thin.

Look for opportunities to create value.

Engage in deliberate practice by sustaining focus and concentration on a task.

Support other tenacious learners by giving less direction and more "figure it out."

Shift your learning disposition and habits to learn at or above the speed of change.

CHAPTER 6

The Second Cornerstone of Competence:

Change

[Humans tend to] seek a state of well-ordered, painless, contented, self-perpetuating equilibrium.

Isaiah Berlin (1909–1997)
Social and political theorist, philosopher, and historian of ideas
"The Intellectual Life of American Universities" (speech, 1949)

Choose Change or Change Will Choose You

Author and journalist Sylvia Nasar wrote, "From the beginning of civilization to the 19th century, 90 percent of humanity was stuck in place, even if their country did comparatively well. Average people lived like livestock—they didn't go anywhere, read anything, or wear much; they ate bad food and didn't live a very long time."[1]

I would not trade centuries with those people, but at least they took some comfort in the familiar. Today we live in a near-constant state of disturbance. We are anything but stuck in place, which makes leadership a more dangerous calling. The principles have not changed, but the conditions have. In education, government, healthcare, and the nonprofit sectors, market upheaval, technological disruption, demographic churning, and political unrest are not going away. Even the hale and hearty must shake hands with radical change here and there. There are no storm-proof organizations, and there are no sources of competitive advantage that last forever. It's all ice. The only question is the rate of the melt.

When this new reality finally registers, you gradually take on a new mind-set, what educator and author Peter Drucker called a *planned abandonment mentality*—a mentality that assumes and anticipates the continuous loss of competitive advantage, a deep psychological acceptance of the turbulence, speed, and complexity of the global age.[2]

Build Your Resilience

It's not enough to acknowledge the turbulence; you have to adjust and adapt to wave after wave of it. Rebounding requires *resilience,* which is the ability to endure and overcome adversity based on tenacious inner motivation. The good news is that resilience to overcome loss, delay, or failure is a learnable skill.[3] Based on accumulated research, we can identify three core characteristics in those with high resilience. They are *confidence, optimism,* and *gratitude*—*COG* for short. Surrounding the core characteristics, leaders apply six additional factors to build resilience: *purpose, relationships, renewal, achievement, contribution,* and *learning.* Those with high resilience tend to apply all of them consistently to sustain and increase their resilience (see figure 6.1):

- Cultivate confidence, optimism, and gratitude

- Find purpose in your work

- Build relationships

- Seek renewal

- Achieve meaningful goals

- Contribute beyond yourself

- Learn at or above the speed of change

Figure 6.1 The Seven-Factor Resilience Model

To gauge your own level of resilience, take the Personal Resilience Assessment (see figure 6.2).

If you gave yourself a score of 1 or 2 on any of the questions, you should consider taking concrete steps to improve your performance in that area. It will have an impact on your overall resilience. If you scored 3, I would offer the same advice. That is a nice, safe score, but only the mediocre are always at their best. Can you do better? The return on investment could catapult you to a whole new level of resilience.

Now consider the mind-set difference between those with high resilience and those with low resilience. As the Personal Resilience Assessment indicates, those with low resilience are on the left side of a bell curve and those with high resilience are on the right (see figure 6.3). Those with low resilience are imprisoned by their mind-set. When dislocating change comes,

Figure 6.2 The Personal Resilience Assessment

N O				Y E S

1. Am I highly driven to achieve my goals?

① ② ③ ④ ⑤

2. Do I know how to renew myself when I am tired or burned out?

① ② ③ ④ ⑤

3. Am I an aggressive, self-directed learner?

① ② ③ ④ ⑤

4. Do I believe I can contribute in a meaningful way?

① ② ③ ④ ⑤

5. Do I have coping mechanisms to avoid feeling overwhelmed?

① ② ③ ④ ⑤

6. Can I laugh at my mistakes and try again?

① ② ③ ④ ⑤

7. Am I flexible, adjusting quickly to changing conditions?

① ② ③ ④ ⑤

8. Am I optimistic, seeing problems as temporary?

① ② ③ ④ ⑤

9. Can I tolerate high levels of uncertainty and ambiguity?

① ② ③ ④ ⑤

10. Do I know how to draw strength from my relationships?

① ② ③ ④ ⑤

11. Am I motivated by the sense of purpose I find in my work?

① ② ③ ④ ⑤

Figure 6.3 The Resilience Spectrum

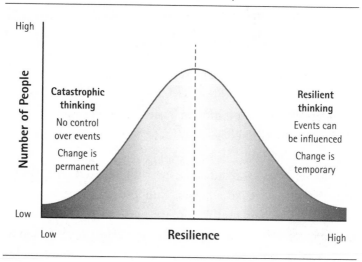

they see it as permanent and out of their control. They engage in what psychologists call "catastrophic thinking." As a result, they become less agile and less able to deal with changing conditions. They withdraw into themselves and sometimes become highly resistant to change if not paralyzed at the prospect of it.

On the other hand, those with high resilience embrace a different mind-set. They believe that conditions can and will change and that they have the power to influence those conditions. Clearly, your mind-set drives your behavior and its results.

Let's run a little scenario to see how you would respond. You are being considered for an important promotion, and you have been told by many people that you are the most qualified candidate and the clear front runner.

The panel of managers making the promotional decision has given you every indication that you will get the job. You come to work the next day. You turn on your computer and log in to your e-mail. At the top of your inbox is a message with the subject line "Thank you for applying." You open the e-mail to find a form letter from the human resources department, thanking you for applying for the position and asking you to schedule an appointment with the HR manager in your division. You can hardly contain your excitement. You call HR and make the appointment for the next day. When you walk into the executive conference room, brimming with confidence and expecting a warm greeting and a promotion, instead you are summarily laid off. Just like that. You have 60 minutes to gather up your things and exit the building.

What would you do? A person with high resilience would be just as devastated as a person with low resilience. But here's the difference: The high-resilience person would move past the hurt, learn from the experience, and get to work on a new opportunity. What would the low-resilience person do? Stay devastated, curl up like a pill bug, fail to act, and sink into a state of deep discouragement.

Remember that resilience grows with use. If our resilience is low, we can find ourselves engaged in a personal battle of denial against the new normal, its pace, and its dynamism. A leader with resilience and a planned abandonment mentality has come to terms with the new reality and has become reconciled to it. Emotional barriers have been permanently disabled.

Do you demonstrate a planned abandonment mentality? Have you made peace with turbulence? Do you realize that there will be times when you need to take bold action to change the way you think and behave? Can you see that there are perverse incentives trying to keep you content right where you are? If you feel yourself slipping into patterns of resistance, resignation, or political expediency, catch yourself. I'm not saying that your career will be one continuous transformational epoch. I am saying that leadership today involves almost constant change, and change in the environment calls forth change in us.

No matter how anticipatory you try to be, there will be blindsided threats that appear without warning. There will be killer applications and disruptive technologies. We cannot divine where the next innovations will come from, but we do know that there will be new breakthroughs. This very day ideas are being incubated, piloted, scaled, and commercialized. What we do know is that every value proposition eventually deadlocks with new threats, and the basis of competition shifts again.

We know it, but it's hard to come to terms with the fact that we must eat change for breakfast. It's hard to look the future in the face. It's uncharted, unscripted, and unknown. And yet we are galloping in that direction. This is both an intellectual and an emotional issue. As a leader you do not necessarily have to be capable of original thought. You do, however, need to be capable of original action.

Do You Smuggle Change or Muscle Change?

As a leader you are supposed to face challenges with purpose, resolve, and speed. At the same time, you're supposed to be collaborative, so you can't rush into change or you might find yourself alone. But wait a second, there's no time for consensus. What do you do? The tendency is to respond in one of two ways: through smuggling or muscling.

Smuggling Change

Leaders who *smuggle* change try to hide what they are doing from the full view of the organization. They try to conceal it, manage it as a covert action, or do it in a corner. The motivation is simple pain avoidance. Unfortunately, this approach usually fails over the long term.

Smugglers assume that change will cause alarm and resistance. Rather than confront those obstacles, they just try to avoid them. The first part of the logic is sound. Change often triggers angst and opposition. But the logic breaks down after that. Successful organizational change is not based on a calm beginning; it's based on a successful outcome, which requires an educated and aligned organization. If you launch your efforts peacefully through a smuggled effort, you have simply delayed, and probably increased, the angst and opposition you tried to avoid. You will have to pay the piper.

Smuggled change efforts are often the ones you don't hear about until the organization bucks later on. For example, at a professional services organization, the accounting department, with full executive support, installed a new system to track consulting travel and expenses. Rather than communicate the change and solicit input from the employees, the department tried to smuggle the effort, thinking it would make it painless and invisible. True to the pattern of a smuggled change, frustration and resistance erupted in all quarters of the organization: "Why wasn't I consulted?" "This new system doesn't do what the old one could do." "The old process wasn't broken." "You should have designed it differently."

In the end the backlash was overwhelming. After several fitful months of trying to make the new system work, the company threw in the towel.

Muscling Change

The second pattern is for leaders to muscle change. *Muscling* is the process of using formal authority and positional power to force change. When you attempt to muscle change through an organization, you are apt to make one of the following assumptions:

- *I know what's best for the organization.*

- *There's no time to discuss it.*

- *You will only resist me anyway.*

■ *You will be convinced only after the fact.*

■ *Organizations respond best to pressure.*

There are elements of truth in all of these assumptions, and leaders who muscle change have often demonstrated impressive results. Gen Y in particular has low tolerance for leaders who want to lead by mandate or rule by fiat.

As a general rule, employees confronted with a muscling leader tend to engage in passive-aggressive behavior, or they simply say good-bye. With the increasing competitiveness of the business environment, and the average CEO tenure in steady decline, employees understand that they can wage wars of attrition with muscling leaders and have a good chance of winning. Like smuggling, the muscling approach to change often yields results in the short term. But over the long term, you suffer the consequences of resistance and widespread employee disengagement.

Why wait for failure? Get to work on your character and competence. Change is tough and often painful, but there is no way around it. Remember, you *manage* resources and *lead* people. Regardless of how beautifully equipped you are in terms of time, resources, and expertise, nothing can compensate for the absence of leadership and the need for inspiration.

Culture by Design or Culture by Default

One of the most important things you can do as a leader is build a resilient and high-performance culture. If I walk into your organization, do I feel lighter and younger or heavier and older? Is the culture energetic or bureaucratic? Is it a *me* or a *we* culture? These are questions you get to ask and answer. You can design your culture or you can let it evolve by default.

Culture is to an organization what habits are to an individual. It's what most people think, believe, say, and do most of the time. When people come together on a regular basis, a culture is born—not immediately but gradually. It's the natural result of interaction. Every organization has a culture. Some are healthy, adaptable, and supportive. Others are toxic, encrusted, and resistant to change. The question is whether you have the culture you want and the culture you need.

Here is the way I like to define culture:

- A pattern of thought or behavior in a person is a *habit*.

- A pattern of thought or behavior in an organization is a *norm*.

- A collection of norms in an organization is a *culture*.

We used to think about culture as a residual category, as a by-product of the organization. And that is true, but we didn't realize that it could be molded to fit the specific vision, mission, and strategy of an organization. Nor did we fully understand how it could be a major strategic asset in directing the way an organization creates value. You should address your culture directly and design it. Culture by default is too dangerous. You run the risk of developing serious cultural liabilities that can hold you back.

When you shape a desired culture, that culture becomes the de facto soft operating system, or the DNA that influences how and at what level the organization performs. Culture shapes an organization's decision patterns, guides its actions, and influences the individual behavior of its members. You get what you design for and consistently reinforce.

Layers of Culture

In most organizations there are three layers of culture. First, there is the institutional or *macroculture*—the culture of the entire organization or enterprise. Second, there are subcultures within the institutional culture; *subcultures* share many of the

Figure 6.4 The Anatomy of Culture

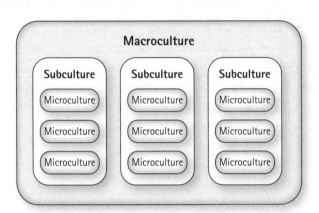

common patterns of the institutional culture, but they also have their own unique patterns. Finally, within the subcultures sit the *microcultures,* which are usually associated with the smallest organizational unit, namely, the team (see figure 6.4).

Once again, the microculture will often share some cultural patterns with the subculture to which it belongs, as well as with the larger macroculture. The point is that in most organizations, it's a favorite pastime to complain about the culture. We like to commiserate, cry in our milk together, and whine about its flaws and dysfunction. That is fine, but when it comes to the micro-culture, complaining is not allowed. You own the microculture. It's your stewardship. It reflects you. We don't whine about our microculture because it's ours. We are responsible to build it, mold it, and shape it into what we need it to be.

Types of Culture

There are two types of culture: visible and invisible. The *visible* layer of culture is what we see in terms of behavior, symbols, tra-ditions, and artifacts. Over time organizations naturally develop common ways of doing things. Our interactions establish prevailing norms in what we say and do. But the outward manifestations of culture are only half the picture. The *invisible* layer of culture refers to what people think, believe, assume, feel, and value. The problem is you can't see this layer of culture. It's below the surface. This subterranean layer precedes the visible layer in terms of sequence. People act and behave based on what they think, believe, assume, feel, and value. Taken together, the invisible and visible layers represent the organization's overall culture. And every organization has one.

Changing Culture

To change your culture, find the things that shape the culture in the first place. Fortunately, the six factors that shape culture are always the same regardless of the industry or organization. The most important culture-building factors have to do with what is modeled, communicated, taught, measured, recognized, and rewarded.

Model What You Want

Of all the factors that shape organizational culture, the single most important one is leadership behavior. Leaders shape culture through modeling. Modeling is simply demonstrated behavior. Organizational cultures do not change unless leadership behavior is manifestly different from the way it has been. Keep in mind that organizations do not perform above their cultures. As the axiom goes, *All organizations are perfectly designed to get the results they get.* What do you want in your culture? Always start with character. Go back to integrity, humility, accountability, and courage. If you are not modeling the four cornerstones of character, your culture will not accidently reflect these attributes.

Of all the aspects of organizational change, changing culture is the most difficult because it is rooted in human thought, belief, and behavior. You should expect a culture change effort to take longer and require more work than other types of organizational change, such as modifications to structure, process, systems, technology, capital assets, cost-cutting, and the like. To shape or change a culture, you must maintain a maniacal focus on what you want in your culture. It will take time, but it will be worth it.

Understand the Context

Another key to leading change in yourself and your organization is to understand your organization's general context. The sector you work in is a big determining factor. Some sectors are inherently more resistant to change than others. If we were to assign a resistance rating using a five-point scale, where 1 is low and 5 is high, the following is what it looks like.

Resistance rating 5: government organizations. On the spectrum of resistance, public-sector institutions earn the highest rating. In this sector poor performance rarely threatens existence because government organizations tend to be far removed from direct accountability. They usually don't need sources of competitive advantage or stakeholder satisfaction to survive. They need only be funded. Take the US Congress, an organization that is frequently paralyzed and unresponsive to stakeholders. Regardless of its performance, it's funded. Therefore it exists. Where direct accountability does not exist, resistance to change thrives.

Resistance rating 4: public educational institutions. Public educational institutions live in a world of monopoly or oligopoly competition with indirect accountability and thick buffers between them and market forces. Our K–12 system is in desperate need of reform, but would-be reformers are ground to dust as the system wages its war of attrition.

The world of public higher education is a little kinder and gentler, but it too is a bastion of tradition and intransigence. I have worked with enough colleges and universities to know that most of them operate on the conviction that they have a right to exist. That is what happens when your organization provides essential services in the absence of strong, direct competition. We can subdivide it further: on balance the private educational institutions move faster and more aggressively, while their public-sector counterparts move at a slower, more lumbering pace.

Resistance rating 3: healthcare institutions. As a whole, the healthcare sector has a history of entrenchment due to low direct accountability and high resistance to change. That has been shifting, though, as competition intensifies. In hospitals, for example, I see more attention and resources given to labor and nonlabor cost reductions, bed management, patient satisfaction, and revenue cycle efficiencies. When I was a student in England, I participated in the British National Health Service. At one point I needed to get a basic physical exam. The health system has some strengths, but speed is not one of them. The wait time was more than two months. I went to a private hospital the next day.

Resistance rating 2: nonprofit organizations. There is one cardinal difference between nonprofit organizations and government, educational, and healthcare institutions: They subsist on private funding. If the funding dries up, they die. This reality tends to imbue nonprofits with a little more agility. They often do not compete on their cost structure, so the operations of many nonprofits are slow and inefficient. If they have good fundraising, they live. The fundraising function is the direct interface of accountability that keeps them hungry and responsive.

Resistance rating 1: business organizations. The private sector is where accountability is most direct and continuous. Businesses die every day. But even here there are subcategories of resistance to change. Basic industry tends to be the most resistant. Industrial organizations are capital intensive and have to invest on multiyear time horizons. Consumer goods are less so, services even less, and the tech sector least of all. The main reason is the length of the product development cycle: the shorter the cycle, the more agile the company.

For example, most of the software companies I work with have abandoned traditional product development cycles in favor of an agile and evergreen approach to development. They have a cadence and a culture that reflect the velocity of the market and the disruptive potential of new entrants.

Making Change Stick

The four *EPIC* stages of organizational change are as follows:

- Evaluation

- Preparation

- Implementation

- Consolidation

The last step, consolidation, means making change stick, which is often the single most difficult part of the change process. For example, I have worked with a number of hospitals, and in every one the issue of infection control is a big priority. As it turns out, nosocomial, or hospital-acquired, infection is a major killer because the hospital environment is in many ways an incubator of infectious disease and its transmission. Bugs can spread in four ways: from patient to patient, from staff to patient, from patient to staff, and from staff to staff. The Centers for Disease Control and

Prevention (CDC) estimates that in the United States 1.7 million hospital-associated infections from all types of bugs combined cause, or are linked to, 99,000 deaths each year.

To control the spread of infection, hospitals have strict and detailed policies and procedures for disinfection, sterilization, and vaccination. But the most important of all these is the simple task of washing your hands. The CDC confirms that the most important measure for preventing the spread of pathogens is effective hand washing. Yet hand washing remains the single biggest obstacle to infection control. In the face of overwhelming urgency, evidence, and motivation, hospitals continue to fight a battle of compliance with their clinical workers on the issue. People forget. They don't have time. They want to avoid the hassle.

To get something to stick, it is helpful to understand the way change roots itself in an organization. Change has to sink, level by level, into the cultural soil. There are three levels of transition a change must pass through before it can stick. If the leader doesn't manage through all three levels, there is always the chance that change will unravel, that people will stop washing their hands (see figure 6.5).

Level 1: technical change. The first level of change is at the technical level. It means putting in place all the nonbehavioral supports for the new behavior. A technical system is a set of mutually reinforcing elements that will help hold the change in place. For hand washing it means establishing the policies and procedures, the training, the modeling, the resources, the communication, the measurement, and the accountability.

Level 2: behavioral change. The second level is behavioral. Change goes to the behavioral level when people begin acting differently under new conditions and with the aid of new or different resources. They are in the system. They are washing their

Figure 6.5 The Three Levels of Change

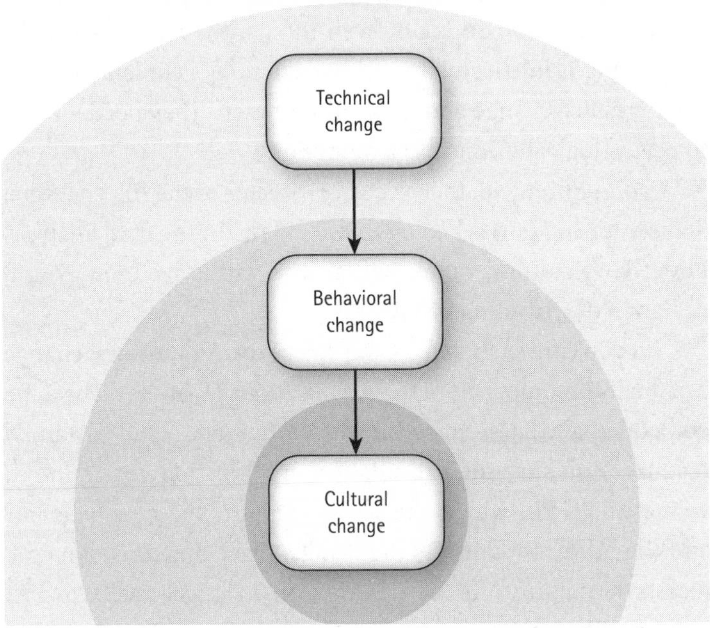

hands when and where they should. By appearances you may think change is here. You have outwardly confirming evidence, right? Don't be fooled. People may not like the new behavior or fully understand it. They may not be convinced of its necessity. They may even resent it. If you took the system away, people would likely regress to the mean and revert to their old behavior.

Level 3: cultural change. The final level is cultural. Unless change finds purchase in people's hearts, it will not last. Over and over I observe that behavior changes before minds do, before hearts do. Humans tend to behave before they believe. Change sticks when the culture finally supports it. By culture I mean the prevailing norms of the organization. In every case, culture changes last. It's the most difficult element to change in any organization because it takes people time to internalize, accept, and support a new behavior emotionally, even though they may already be supporting it intellectually and behaviorally. People need time to internalize change and make it their own. They need a while to psychologically adjust to a new reality.

John Ehrenfeld, the executive director of the International Society for Industrial Ecology, concludes, "In the final analysis, underlying cultural values will always trump technology and design in determining behavior."[4]

If you consistently feed and starve the right things, change eventually becomes part of the organization's DNA. It will become embedded and internalized in the culture and yield sustained results. With sustained results the organization enters into a virtuous cycle in which the results support the new behavior and the behavior supports the results. Over time this dynamic recasts the culture until the organization no longer reverts to past patterns. There's new muscle memory.

CHANGE: SUMMARY POINTS

Adopt a planned abandonment mentality.

Develop greater resilience by applying seven factors:

- ◆ *COG: Confidence, optimism, and gratitude*
- ◆ *Purpose*
- ◆ *Relationships*
- ◆ *Renewal*
- ◆ *Achievement*
- ◆ *Contribution*
- ◆ *Learning*

Do not smuggle or muscle change.

Change culture by design not by default.

Take complete ownership of your microculture.

Model the culture you want.

Make change stick by moving through the three layers of change:

- ◆ *Level 1: Technical change*
- ◆ *Level 2: Behavioral change*
- ◆ *Level 3: Cultural change*

Behave until you believe.

CHAPTER 7

The Third Cornerstone of Competence:

Judgment

A decision is a judgment. It is a choice between alternatives.
It is rarely a choice between right and wrong. It is at best a choice
between "almost right" and "probably wrong"—but much
more often a choice between two courses of action neither
of which is provably more nearly right than the other.

Peter F. Drucker (1909–2005)
Austrian-born American management consultant, educator, and author
Management: Tasks, Responsibilities, and Practices (1993)

Seeing the Big Picture

In 1952 a group of renowned scientists gathered at the Massachusetts Institute of Technology for what would become known as the Summer Study Group. In the background Cold War tensions were escalating between the United States and the Soviet Union. What concerned national security experts most was the possibility that Moscow could dispatch long-range bombers armed with nuclear warheads and send them over the polar region undetected. In response the US government commissioned its scientists to make a detailed study of North American vulnerability to such an attack. Out of the deliberations came an urgent recommendation to build a distant early-warning system—what became known as the DEW Line—consisting of state-of-the-art radar stations arrayed across the Arctic Circle.

Under the guidance of a bilateral agreement, the US and Canadian governments joined forces and commenced the project. After less than three years of construction, an integrated chain of 63 radar stations dotted the landscape 200 miles north of the Arctic Circle and stretching 3,000 miles from Alaska to Canada's Baffin Island. The DEW Line represented the world's most advanced detection system, an engineering and logistical marvel, and the cornerstone of North American air defense.

But here's the irony: The DEW Line was rendered obsolete almost as soon as it was built. The project was commissioned in July 1957, and the very next month Soviet scientists pulled off a game-changing move: they successfully test-fired the R7—the world's first intercontinental ballistic missile (ICBM). It would take only two more years for the Soviets to deploy a military ICBM, allowing them to launch a nuclear attack from their home turf. With astonishing speed, new realities had thwarted the much-vaunted new intelligence-gathering capability. So much for the DEW Line.

Today the business ecosystem goes well beyond the traditional boundaries of home markets, direct competition, and current customers. Leaders need an extended field of vision. Certainly, leaders must rely on judgment and make business decisions somewhere short of certainty. But too many leaders still take the intolerably high risk of relying on scant data, anecdotal information, and impressionistic evidence when a great deal more information is available. Decisions are only as good as the intelligence that informs them.

When I do strategy work with organizations, I ask leaders to back up and look at their intelligence-gathering process first. Here are some questions to consider:

- How do you conduct market reconnaissance?

- How systematic or haphazard is your process for scanning the competitive landscape?

- How do you spot early signs of opportunity and pending risk?

- Do you have an integrated framework to help you gather, aggregate, and interpret information from a variety of sources that might bear on the organization's competitive position?

- Does your strategic-planning process account for the complex interplay of factors and the heightened uncertainty of the business ecosystem?

Harvard psychologist Howard Gardner argues that leaders need synthesizing minds that see connections among fragments of knowledge. The challenge is that this need for "searchlight intelligence," as he terms it, is not enough given the sheer volume of information that must be filtered, synthesized, and made actionable.[1] Organization consultants and educators Warren Bennis and Noel Tichy claim that leadership is "the chronicle of judgment calls."[2]

So, I challenge you to take a hard look at the way you gather and make sense of the information around you. Is your current approach a vestige of a more stable postwar era? Remember, poor intelligence produces blinkered thinking, which yields poor decisions. As the speed of change hastens and the average span of competitive advantage shortens, leaders must be able to spot the earliest signs of change, anticipate market movements, calculate potential disruptions, and prepare for their arrival.

It all goes back to judgment. And what is judgment? It's the sifting, sorting, filtering, and connecting of information, logic, values, and objectives. It's thinking through different courses

Figure 7.1 The Complexity of Judgment

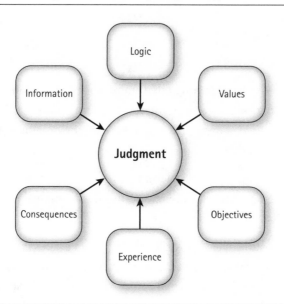

of action. It's thinking through first-, second-, and third-order consequences. Finally, it's about making the call (see figure 7.1).

Systems Thinking

Researchers have a fancy name for being able to see all the parts and pieces that go into making a decision, especially a hard one. They call it *systems thinking*. It's true that some people seem to have a natural gift for seeing a complex, dynamic system holistically; considering the interaction of the constituent parts; and thinking through different courses of action. This is a huge aspect of judgment, but you can significantly improve your ability to do this. The basic principle is this: more complexity means more ambiguity. If there are more moving parts, there are more ways for those parts to interact (see figure 7.2).

Figure 7.2 The Complexity and Ambiguity of Systems

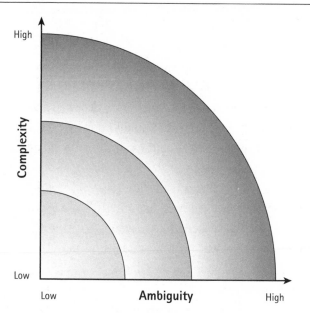

The figure illustrates how both complexity and ambiguity increase as you move to a bigger system. There is no getting around the principle.

"Victor" Analysis

Regardless of how challenging it may be to synthesize and distill information, exercise judgment, and make a decision, in almost every case there are four fundamental criteria you must address. In most cases, good judgment is based on a careful simultaneous analysis of all four of them. I call it the *VCTR* (pronounced "victor") *model:*

- **Value:** What value results from this course of action?

- Cost: What are the costs of this course of action?

- **Time:** What time is required for this course of action?

- **Risk:** What are the risks of this course of action?

If you can consistently adopt the discipline of looking at these four criteria for almost any decision, you will develop better judgment over time. And it really doesn't matter the scope, scale, magnitude, duration, or significance of the decision: Should I buy this car? Should I take this job? Should I donate to this charity? Should I read this book? Should I call this unhappy customer back today or tomorrow? A VCTR analysis does not tell you what to do; it gives you a clear way to frame your thinking.

Sometimes you will have quantitative data available, and sometimes you won't. Remember, even when you do, the data may point to the answer, but you still have to make the decision. Judgment is a combination of data, logic, gut, and inspiration. It's never easy. It's never formulaic. The point is that you must consult every source and then boil down an answer for each criterion.

Adaptive Challenge

Judgment is about interpreting what is not yet obvious. Venture capitalist and former co-founder of Netscape Marc Andreessen notes, "Big breakthrough ideas often seem nuts the first time you see them."[3] One way to look at things is to view them based on three categories of *adaptive challenge:* the opportunity, the threat, and the crisis.

- An **opportunity** is an adaptive challenge that offers potential benefit to you, the team, or the organization and that presents no potential harm.

- A **threat** offers potential harm and no potential benefit.

- A **crisis** offers certain harm.

With opportunities, you must interpret emerging and probable forces and their likely impacts. With threats, you have to respond to imminent danger. And with crisis, you must confront the reality that a crisis has struck.

Opportunities come in two varieties: "far and foggy" and "close and clear." Far and foggy opportunities are distantly separated from the organization and naturally offer a low level of clarity. They conceal potential gain, making it a greater risk for a leader to respond early. Circumstances are underdeveloped. Outcomes are uncertain. We are looking at possibilities rather than facts. High uncertainty always keeps an opportunity in a state of low market demand. As a result, responding to far and foggy opportunities can be either genius or folly.

The global financial meltdown was caused in part by sophisticated financial institutions gorging on collateralized debt obligations laden with subprime mortgages. Why? Because the securities appeared to represent a promising investment opportunity—a far and foggy one. In this particular case, the opportunity was tempting. Not certain how to assess and manage this elevated class of risk, many experienced investors proceeded without understanding how it all worked. Others saw it as a signal to avoid.

As economist and professional investor Benjamin Graham cautioned, "Have the courage of your knowledge and experience. If you have formed a conclusion from the facts and if you know your judgment is sound, act on it—even though others may hesitate or differ. (You are neither right nor wrong because the crowd disagrees with you…)."[4]

Most opportunities tend to be far and foggy. Distance shrouds potential rewards, and yet some see potential rewards in the same uncertainty. Once an opportunity becomes equally visible to competitors, potential rewards diminish or are lost altogether. For example, a first mover may exploit an underserved market and accrue substantial rewards initially, but those rewards will dilute as competitors move in. With the categories of adaptive challenge in mind, let me explain two common patterns and one rare one.

Linear Migration

Some adaptive challenges follow a pattern in which they start as an opportunity, become a threat, and then finally become a crisis. Here is a simple example: A member of your team is a highly productive project manager, produces high-quality work very fast, and then spends the rest of the day surfing the Internet. There's an opportunity to give her a challenging assignment and increase her contribution. You do nothing. She gets bored and restless. Now it's a threat. She starts taking two-hour lunches, which affects morale. You still do nothing. This exceptionally talented person leaves the company at exactly the wrong time. Your poor timing just cost you big-time. Is procrastination a legitimate leadership principle? Almost never. Unless you are waiting for critical information, act before circumstances conspire against you.

Fleeting Appearance

A second pattern involves an adaptive challenge that appears briefly as an opportunity and then vanishes. Whereas some adaptive challenges begin at the periphery as far and foggy opportunities that continue an inbound trajectory toward the organization, others appear briefly as close and clear opportunities and then disappear altogether. This pattern is based on a nonrepeating combination of timing and circumstance. Unless exploited to competitive advantage, fleeting appearances are usually lost forever. For example, in February 2008 Yahoo CEO Jerry Yang refused a $47.5 billion offer from Microsoft.[5] The company is now up for auction, its core businesses are worth about $2 billion as of this writing, Yang is no longer CEO, and the opportunity is gone.

Sudden Disruption

Finally, an adaptive challenge can appear suddenly as a threat or even a crisis, with no early-warning signs. Think about the Kennedy assassination, 9/11, Hurricane Katrina, the collapse of Lehman Brothers, and terrorist attacks.

Judgment in Timing

Legendary baseball player Ted Williams once said, "Waiting for the right pitch is the most important thing for a batter."[6] What is true in baseball is true in life and leadership: Brilliant moves are based on timing. So are fateful miscalculations. Always remember this principle: the problems you do not solve offensively you will eventually have to solve defensively.

When leaders make decisions, it's not just a matter of *what* but of *when*. Timing is critical because it implies tradeoffs, and leaders, as economist and researcher Michael Porter states, are the "guardians of tradeoffs."[7] It's not enough to know what to do. Deciding when to do it can often be just as important. In fact, timing can be the very thing, and sometimes the only thing, that makes a decision right. Besides the decision itself, there are always two opportunities to get it wrong: acting too early and acting too late. Leaders often fail to appreciate the tradeoffs of timing.

To continue with the baseball analogy, the first thing is to figure out when the ball will arrive. Leaders are in the business of responding to stimuli—some good, some bad, some unknown. If you are a leader, think of yourself at the plate with a bat in your hands. The pitches are coming one after another. Your job is to decide which ones to swing at and when. Step one is to figure out the point of impact, be it an opportunity, a threat, or a crisis. When will the challenge arrive? When should you start your swing—or should you swing at all? Is it a fastball at 94 miles per hour or a knuckleball at 74?

There are inherent tradeoffs based on the speed and pattern of the ball. Consider the five factors of timing:

- Clarity
- Urgency
- Response time
- Available options
- Margin for error

With a better understanding of these dimensions, you will be better prepared to make the right choice at the right time. You will not bat 1,000, but you'll improve your batting average.

To assess your timing in responding to an adaptive challenge, answer the following questions.

How clear is the adaptive challenge you are responding to? The closer the ball is to your bat, the better you can tell if it's the pitch you want. Did you know that swinging the bat in the wrong place is *not* the biggest batting mistake in baseball? It's simply starting the swing too late. Similarly, leaders are prone to delay or fail to respond to opportunities because they cannot see them clearly enough, and they don't want to deal with the uncertainty. It is easier to commit later to what is real than to commit early to what might be real.

At what level of urgency must the organization respond? The urgency associated with a pitch follows the same pattern as clarity. Urgency is usually based on high clarity. The closer that nice pitch, the more urgently we want to swing. Similarly, low clarity is almost always accompanied by low urgency. There is very little urgency between pitches, so we tap our cleats and take a practice swing. The next pitch is an opportunity on the far horizon. That explains why preemptive strategic moves are almost never made based on current reality. What level of urgency do you have between pitches? It's low because the point of impact is far away.

How much time do you have to respond? The closer the pitch, the shorter the response time. When leaders allow pitches to move closer, they assume a higher risk of failure. If the batter hesitates to begin the swing for even a split second, the opportunity is gone. Fortunately, organizational life is not a game of seconds, but the principle holds true. Procrastination is a legitimate business principle. Just make sure you're using it to your advantage.

What options are available to you to respond? Available options also flex with the point of impact. If you have a little time, you have the luxury to test a variety of response options. With a threat those options narrow, given the shorter time horizon. Finally, in a crisis leaders often find themselves constrained to only one option because time has run out. When it's a full count and you're staring at the pitcher, your strategic options have been narrowed without your permission. If the count is three balls and no strikes, you can try for a bunt, swing for the fences, or just get a base hit.

What is the margin for error? Finally, less time means less margin for error. Back to the full-count scenario: you've got no more strikes, so give that next pitch a ride or hit the dugout.

Judgment in Selecting People

Management guru Jim Collins exhorts leaders to get the right people on the bus, but it's actually an old admonition. In the Old Testament, we encounter a case study of someone who failed to follow this counsel. The verse reads: "Abimelech hired vain and light persons, which followed him."[8]

These nine words point to a critical area of judgment for all leaders: judging people, their talents, and their potential. Why are leaders tempted to surround themselves with sycophants and flatterers? To do so is to eat Twinkies at every meal. It does nothing for you.

And yet history is replete with stories of leaders who assembled galleries of pandering, fawning, doting, gushing, and servile courtiers to stroke their egos. What does an assemblage of obsequious followers have to do with leadership? Exactly nothing. The unsavory British monarch King Henry VIII had his counselor, Sir Thomas More, executed. More may have been vain, but he was not light, so he could not stay. A milder form of this temptation is simply to hire mediocre or low performers. You have heard it said that A's hire A's and B's hire C's. There is a lot of truth to that. And why is that? Because, as Antoine de Saint-Exupéry wrote in *The Little Prince*, "To vain men, other people are admirers."[9] So, they go off looking for their biggest fans.

It is fascinating that the two greatest presidents in American history tried very hard to get the right people on the bus, to the point that their cabinets were at times dysfunctional and threatened their presidencies. Both men hired vain persons but not light persons. They surrounded themselves with the most capable people. The problem of course is that the most capable people are often besotted with ego and ambition. These presidents assembled teams with more chance of success and yet more risk of failure.

George Washington came to office with 100 percent of the nation's electoral vote—a clear and unassailable mandate that no president since has enjoyed. To govern he knew he needed to enlist the best talent he could find. In retrospect you could argue that the bitter feud over national credit between Alexander

Hamilton, the first secretary of the treasury, and Thomas Jefferson, the first secretary of state, was so debilitating that it did not serve the nation. That remains a point of debate.

We do know that strong-minded rather than like-minded people tend to engage and contend more aggressively for turf and influence. That is not necessarily a good thing, but it's better than having shrinking violets who can't make a significant contribution in the first place. Washington knew that and was willing to bear the added burden of managing egos and refereeing disputes. It was better than a team of yes-men.

Abraham Lincoln won the hotly contested presidential election of 1860. His political foes—William H. Seward, Salmon P. Chase, and Edward Bates—were bruised and resentful. It required enormous personal sacrifice to invite those men into his cabinet. Lincoln took them, knowing that they would be high risk and high maintenance, and they did not disappoint. They would often work against him, defy him, and at times try to subvert his authority, his decisions, and his credibility. I'm not suggesting that he made all the right calls. Some of the behavior he had to deal with, such as Chase's repeated threats to resign, was simply insufferable. But in the end, he drew from each a measurable and significant contribution, and that is why he tolerated their disloyalty and absorbed their bickering.

A leader's judgment in talent selection reveals much. John W. Gardner, a member of Lyndon Johnson's cabinet, said of judgment, "Most importantly, perhaps, it includes the capacity to appraise the potentialities of co-workers (and opponents)."[10]

If you happen to be in a position of selecting and hiring people, and if we were to analyze you as a leader strictly on the basis of your hiring and promotion decisions, what would we learn? Niccolo Machiavelli, the Renaissance writer and advocate of realpolitik, wrote, "The first method for estimating the intelligence of a ruler is to look at the men he has around him."[11] Your team reflects your judgment.

Judgment in Developing People

Developing people is at the very center of leadership. At some point we awaken to the unfortunate reality that we cannot simply express our wishes and expect them to be carried out. Unless you work exclusively with hungry, self-starting, perpetually motivated, and universally competent people, you will come to know that delegation among mere mortals is a skill of the highest order. It is the key to building your bench and your future. When I first became a manager, I held a staff meeting, made some assignments, dispatched my direct reports, and then sat back thinking about my grand vision. We met again the next week. Can you guess what happened? Nothing happened.

It all begins with a proper understanding of the delegation principle: Leaders should delegate everything they possibly can—and I mean everything—while prudently managing risk. If others can perform the work within an acceptable margin of error and with the guidance, resources, and accountability you have available, let them do it. If you think delegation is expensive, try micromanagement. This goes back to humility. Remember that humility is an acknowledgment of your ignorance and dependency on others. No one is omnicompetent. You share work with others for two reasons: to get needed help and to help others grow. When we do not delegate, we usually think we can do something faster or better. That may be true in the short term, but over the long term you are stuck.

Delegation does two things. First, you multiply force and increase overall contribution. Second, you accelerate the development of other people. Your job is to stretch people and make demands of them, not coddle them, and do it in a way that builds confidence and capacity. To maximize the opportunity for others to grow, you withhold nothing that you do not absolutely have to do yourself. In the short run, it takes more time and energy. In the long run, you find yourself surrounded by more leaders and more capability. This might sound overly aggressive, but you never cut yourself loose from managing risk or developing people. When you delegate, give people all they can handle but no more. They will progress from individual tasks to tactical projects to strategic outcomes.

Proper delegation means providing direction, training, vision, and encouragement at the front end. It also means providing measurement and accountability at the back end. Delegation is never abdication. You never walk away. And you never stop managing risk. Most people prefer the front end of delegation; there's a fun factor. We dislike the back end; there's a fear factor—the fear of confrontation. This is where we often shrink.

If you delegate a task and the person fails to complete it properly, first find the cause. Was it skill or will? Was it the result of an ability problem or a motivation problem? The two failure patterns are different and require different responses. Did failure result from willfulness, negligence, or a good-faith effort? If a person fails willfully, he meant to. There should be a consequence for that. If a person fails out of negligence, it's still an act of will rather than a lack of skill, but you will have to look deeper to really understand the underlying reasons. Finally, if a person fails in spite of a good-faith effort, the motivation is still there. You know that person is trying.

A willful failure is never acceptable. Before you rush to judgment, however, make sure you analyze the person's initial response. If a person commits a willful failure and responds with denial, blame, or excuse, you cannot pass Go. There is no progress until there is acknowledgment and ownership of one's actions. And in this case, the main purpose of a consequence is to produce personal ownership.

Failure due to negligence is a tough one because it often involves a root cause that's a combination of motivation and ability. People often fail simply because they don't try. There's a lack of confidence behind the inaction. My advice is to analyze carefully, be gentle, err on the side of leniency, and spend your time encouraging and building confidence. When a person fails out of good faith, it's more often a victory than a failure. It means they were in it to win it. They did their best. In time it is effort that will trump all other considerations. If there's consistent effort, the consequences will eventually take care of themselves.

Leadership is about performance and development—what you do and whom you leave behind. When leaders create dependency through micromanagement, they miss the entire point. When they leave a legacy of capable leaders, they become students of leverage and make their fullest contribution. If a leader doesn't learn to delegate effectively, that leader will simply not progress, and those under his charge will become frustrated and disengaged. Leadership depends on the principles of delegation and accountability—the process of dividing work, assigning it to others, and having them give account of their performance.

Affiliation and Accountability

To develop greater judgment and effectiveness in helping others perform and progress, keep two factors in mind: affiliation and accountability. *Affiliation* refers to your ability to cultivate and maintain strong relationships with others. *Accountability* means you make people answerable for the responsibilities you delegate to them. Four different combinations are possible, represented by four quadrants (see figure 7.3). These quadrants represent patterns that I see in leaders everywhere. Three of the four patterns are dysfunctional and reflect poor judgment by the leader. Let me briefly explain each.

Figure 7.3 The Clark Accountability Model

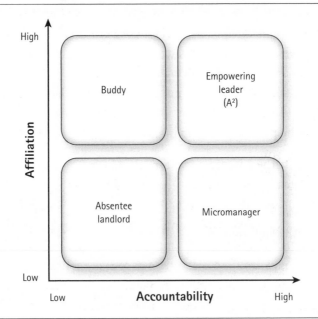

Pattern 1: The buddy. Look at the upper-left quadrant. The buddy profile is a leader who usually builds strong relationships with people (high affiliation) but does not hold them strictly account-able for their performance (low accountability). We often see this profile in sales organizations, where a sales manager connects well with the team but hesitates when there's a performance issue. Leaders in the "buddy box" want to be liked and shrink from the task of holding others accountable. Relationships rank higher than responsibility. They mistakenly believe that if they hold someone accountable, it will ruin the relationship.

Holding another person accountable at the moment of truth requires managerial courage. As a Fortune 500 CEO once said to me, "Many leaders simply don't have the emotional maturity and confidence to have an adult conversation with another person and say, 'I really like you as a person, but this level of performance is unacceptable.'" Organizations often develop a "make nice" pattern of accepting poor performance from their employees. With time the pattern stirs resentment in high performers. People start believing they have a right *not* to be held accountable. They can become offended when called to account. In the end we realize that we have done a disservice to ourselves and to the person who should have been held accountable.

Pattern 2: The absentee landlord. The lower-left quadrant combines low affiliation and low accountability. It is the home of the absentee landlord. The attitude of the absentee landlord is *I'm not there and I don't care.* Control is not the guiding impulse for the absentee landlord but rather freedom from responsibility. The absentee landlord delegates but does not follow up. It's my observation that most absentee landlords live under the false assumption that organizations can run themselves and that high performance can be self-executing. Or they are simply checked out. It's excruciatingly painful to be led by an absentee landlord because, for people who are striving, no criticism at all is the hardest thing to bear.

Pattern 3: The micromanager. Next is the lower-right quadrant, the micromanager. The micromanager is the leader who refuses to delegate and empower, marked by low affiliation and high accountability. Logically, we micromanage when we do not have confidence that another person can do the job. But if a person can do the job, why would we still micromanage her? Either we are insecure in our ability to give up control, or we cling to it out of overabundant ego. In either case, we retard growth, breed dependency, and send a clear signal of no confidence.

From his experience in taking over command of the USS *Benfold,* Captain D. Michael Abrashoff admonishes, "Leaders must free their subordinates to fulfill their talents to the utmost. However, most obstacles that limit people's potential are set in motion by the leader and are rooted in his or her own fears, ego needs, and unproductive habits. When leaders explore deep within their thoughts and feelings in order to understand themselves, a transformation can take shape."[12]

Pattern 4: The empowering leader. The fourth category is a combination of high affiliation and high accountability, or what I call the empowering leader. As I observe leaders around the world, the most effective ones demonstrate this clear pattern. To develop their people, they do two things.

First, they cultivate a genuine personal relationship with the person they are helping develop. They throw out the conventional wisdom of maintaining professional distance because the concept is false. Instead they really get to know their people. They have high affiliation with their people, meaning a strong connection and bond of friendship. Out of that friendship grows a sense of stewardship and desire to invest in their development. Second, they hold their people accountable. They expect them to perform and they follow up to ensure that they do. If there are challenges along the way, they help. This combination of high affiliation and high accountability creates an exponential effectiveness, or A^2.

Judgment and Success

As you improve in judgment, you will ultimately become more successful simply because a higher percentage of your decisions will be right. Unfortunately, the opposite relationship can also be true: the more successful you become, the worse your judgment. We call this the *curse of success*. What is particularly dangerous is when you succeed in your first attempt at anything. There's a good chance you will not understand why. You can't discern which factors accounted for your success. You may attribute it to your own brilliance, but you still have a far-too-general hypothesis. This often happens with entrepreneurs who hit it big on their first try and are serial failures after that.

Here is the pattern:

- Success leads to arrogance.

- Arrogance leads to impaired judgment.

- Impaired judgment leads to error.

- Error leads to failure.

Warren Buffett once observed, "A fat wallet is the enemy of superior investment results."[13] The fatness of that wallet tends to produce hubris in the investor, and it is no different for any other leader. Success is seductive and sedative. It can quietly rob you of judgment. It can breed arrogance, insensitivity, and willful blindness. You start to see yourself and your business with unwarranted optimism. And our society does not necessarily help.

As MIT professor Edgar Schein puts it, "Our culture emphasizes that leaders must be wiser, set direction, and articulate values, all of which predisposes them to tell rather than ask."[14] The final result is that you begin to ignore warnings. This leads to poor judgment, and poor judgment leads to more errors.

In the high-velocity environment of the twenty-first century, success can simply get you into trouble faster. As a form of confirming evidence, it says you know what you're doing. It beguiles us into believing that we can simply replicate the success of the past. I see this with many leaders. What is even more dangerous than success is sustained success. The longer the track record of achievement, the thicker the complacency, the narrower the mind-set, and the more unfounded the confidence in future success.

Organizational psychologists Karl Weick and Kathleen Sutcliffe make a penetrating observation of this principle: "Success narrows perceptions, changes attitudes, feeds confidence in a single way of doing business, breeds overconfidence in the efficacy of current abilities and practices, and makes leaders and others intolerant of opposing points of view."[15] Success makes us less open to feedback, disconfirming evidence, and alternative points of view. Our ego defenses get in the way. I know several leaders who are surrounded by capable people and yet suffer from isolation. Their people have stopped giving them counsel when it was no longer appreciated. What can you do? Start by asking yourself some penetrating questions (see figure 7.4).

If you gave yourself a score of 3 or less on any question, take some time to ponder your personal pattern and discuss it with someone you trust. Then ask yourself, *Could this pattern limit my ability to exercise good judgment?* You will know what to do after that.

Figure 7.4 The Judgment Cultivation Self-Assessment

NO				YES

1. Do I recognize that valuable insight can come from unlikely people?

① ② ③ ④ ⑤

2. Am I emotionally advanced beyond needing to hear myself talk?

① ② ③ ④ ⑤

3. Do I encourage people to debate issues on their merits?

① ② ③ ④ ⑤

4. Do I get defensive when people challenge me?

① ② ③ ④ ⑤

5. Am I as curious as I used to be?

① ② ③ ④ ⑤

6. Do I ask enough questions?

① ② ③ ④ ⑤

7. Do I avoid cynicism and sarcasm?

① ② ③ ④ ⑤

8. Do I have a habit of thanking those who have helped me be successful?

① ② ③ ④ ⑤

9. Do I value the opinions of those who have no power or position?

① ② ③ ④ ⑤

10. Do I listen solely with the intent to comprehend?

① ② ③ ④ ⑤

JUDGMENT: SUMMARY POINTS

Look at the big picture in two ways:

◆ *First, see a complex, dynamic system holistically.*

◆ *Second, see it over time to spot potential unintended consequences.*

Think through the implications of different courses of action.

Apply the VCTR model to your decisions. Consider:

◆ *Value*   ◆ *Cost*   ◆ *Time*   ◆ *Risk*

View adaptive challenges in three categories:

◆ *Opportunity*   ◆ *Threat*   ◆ *Crisis*

The problems you do not solve offensively you will eventually have to solve defensively.

Consider the inherent tradeoffs of timing based on these five factors:

◆ *Clarity*   ◆ *Urgency*   ◆ *Response time*

◆ *Available options*   ◆ *Margin for error*

Surround yourself with talented, strong-minded people rather than mediocre like-minded people.

Exercise judgment in developing people by combining high affiliation and high accountability.

At all costs resist the arrogance and overconfidence that can come with success.

CHAPTER 8

The Fourth Cornerstone of Competence:

Vision

Make no little plans; they have no magic to stir men's blood and probably themselves will not be realized. Make big plans; aim high in hope and work.

Daniel Hudson Burnham (1846–1912)
American architect and urban designer
Quoted in *Daniel H. Burnham, Architect, Planner of Cities* (1921)

The Ability to See

The fourth and final cornerstone of competence is vision. I want to focus mainly on personal vision—to have vision to see what does not exist, to see what others cannot see, and to see potential and possibility in both yourself and others. A vision is a seedling of reality, a portrait of the future, a life-giving force. It taps mental, emotional, spiritual, and physical energy and propels you forward. It is both a catalyst to start and a sustainer to continue.[1]

A vision points to the future. Even a crude, opaque hint of your potential can be enormously motivating. When you gain a personal vision of what you can become, that internal sense of a future state changes behavior. That unseen impression or mental engraving of your potential draws you forward. Leaders do this for others. They see what you can't see in yourself, and they carry that vision for you until you can lift your gaze. Your vision will increase as your confidence grows because vision and confidence grow together. That is what leaders do. They have done it for you, and now you must do it for others.

Visions Are Not Dreams

Here is a corollary principle: vision is more than sight alone. It's sight with a muscular commitment behind it. There is a crucial distinction here between having a vision and having a mere dream. Authors James Champy and Nitin Nohria claim that "most dreams are stillborn."[2] That is true. Most dreams are stillborn because they are passive and idle thoughts. They are just ideas, and, as we all know, ideas are a dime a dozen. Being dreamy is being slack with no intention to act.

How do you know if your idea is a vision or a dream? There's an easy way to find out. First ask yourself, *Do I want to achieve it?* That is the easy question. Now here's the hard one: *Am I willing to achieve it?* Don't answer too quickly. Count the cost. This is the question that separates a vision from a dream. One of my daughters not only wants to be a great soccer player but is also willing to work to achieve it. When she was first learning how to juggle a soccer ball, she would practice in the backyard. She would come in, dripping sweat, and say, "Hey, Dad, guess how many times I juggled!"

"How many?"

"Sixteen times," she would say.

Time went by, and then one day she came into the house, dripping, and said, "Dad, guess how many times I juggled!"

"How many?"

"One thousand and sixty-nine," she said.

Wanting to do it had something to do with it. Being willing to do it had everything to do with it.

To test your vision about something, you have to test your resolve and willingness to make it happen. Here is an example of the wanting/willing gap: My consulting company conducted a survey of employees in more than 60 organizations. We asked if they wanted to be promoted. Roughly 50 percent of those surveyed said they did. Then we asked if they were willing to develop the skills and knowledge necessary to be promoted. Only 25 percent indicated that they were. Wanting something is an idle dream. Everybody wants stuff. Being willing to work for something is evidence of real vision. When I was a kid, I had two friends. One wanted to be a physician. The other was willing to become a physician. Guess who the physician is today?

Vision Helps You Survive

Vision has a second purpose. It not only fuels your ambition and helps you become and achieve more; it also helps you survive when adversity strikes, when life slams you with a trial you were not expecting. Early in our marriage, Tracey and I were expecting our first child. We were both overwhelmed and yet overjoyed at the prospect of becoming parents. About seven months into our pregnancy, I lost my job. I remember going to the bank to get a loan so that we could pay the hospital bill to have the baby.

"Do you have any collateral you can pledge for the loan?" asked the loan officer at the bank.

"Yes, I have two cases of ramen," I said. No, I did not really say that, but I wanted to. I convinced the bank to loan me the money anyway. I told Tracey not to have the baby until I got a job. She didn't comply. The baby came. It was a glorious time.

But the terror came back. The days turned into weeks, and the weeks turned into months and still no job. I was getting desperate, but then I would hold my son. When I looked at him, it infused me with vision—a vision of his life and my stewardship to take care of him. I clung to that vision in those days. It helped me resist discouragement and keep fighting. The economy was in the tank, so I eventually got a job that paid slightly above minimum wage. Eventually, things got better.

I don't like to think about those days, but it's important to understand that vision helps us survive when thriving is not an option. Social psychologist Erich Fromm said, "Uncertainty is the very condition to impel man to unfold his powers."[3] I think he's half right. Uncertainty alone can immobilize you. Uncertainty mixed with vision can mobilize you. It's the vision that lifts you out of crisis and pushes you forward to a brighter day.

Vision Comes from Identity

Another powerful source of vision is your identity. Specifically, I'm referring to your intergenerational identity as a product of your family's heritage. A sense of where you came from can steel you to face the future. People feel this intuitively. How else do you explain the massive surge in the popularity of genealogy across the United States that has accompanied the development of Internet technology? Ancestral research now ranks as the nation's second most popular hobby next to gardening because it offers intellectual, emotional, and spiritual rewards. It offers the thrill of discovery and unfolds a vision of who you are. People are naturally driven to seek out their heritage. As they learn about their ancestors, they come to understand themselves. A vision of your origin gives you a vision of your future possibilities based on a unifying narrative of your lineage.[4]

Before you can supply vision to others, you need a vision of your own life. If you are struggling to find that vision, may I suggest that you dig into your family history. Find out where you come from and who you come from. As you do this, look for accounts of ancestors who overcame challenges and setbacks in their lives. Stories that reveal the character of your ancestors will speak to you and help reveal your own character. That is the flashpoint: When we learn how an ancestor overcame a trial, we look in the mirror and see past ourselves. We gain an extended and overarching vision of who we are. We become deeply motivated to do things we did not think possible.

Let me give you an example. I recently came into possession of a three-page personal history of my grandfather, Wallace Christofferson, something we never knew existed. For the first time in my life, I had the chance to read about his life in his own words.

Grandpa was orphaned by age six. Being the youngest of nine children, he was passed around the extended family. Finally, at the age of 15, he said he was 18 and joined the US Army during World War I. After the war he took up boxing and had a match with Jack Dempsey, the heavyweight champion of the world. He did not fare too well, but he did say he was proud of the scar Dempsey gave him over his eye. He married my grandmother during the depths of the Great Depression. Grandpa would search for work wherever he could find it, sleeping on park benches, moving from town to town. They lost their first two babies at birth due to lack of proper nourishment.

In the end, he overcame the perils and setbacks of his life and became a dedicated family man, a loyal friend, and a servant to all. He became a leader. He tasted the bitter without becoming bitter.

How do you think this makes me feel? It charges me with a vision of who I am. It gives me strength and determination. If Grandpa could come out on top after all that, what on earth is my excuse? I have a sense of my intergenerational self. I have a vision of the future because I know the past. Where you came from can provide both vision and the enduring motivation to achieve it.

The Importance of Galactic Vision

Now let's open the aperture and talk about vision on a grand scale. Specifically, I want to talk about the real bones of the narrative of

Steve Jobs because it's instructive for everyone. Let me focus on what I believe was his most defining feature: vision. I'm talking about *galactic vision*. It's a characteristic that is not as prevalent in humans as you would think, or at least it lies dormant in most of us. Jobs had it in abundance from the beginning.

"Don't be trapped by dogma," he said. "Don't let the noise of others' opinions drown out your own inner voice."[5] Strong personalities have this quality of independence. The question is what to do with it, how to give it expression. Jobs was bound to influence a lot and be influenced a little. He was born an independent variable—a cause rather than an effect.

Jobs had many faults. He often treated people poorly and did not learn to give freely of himself. I don't hold him up as a mentor, coach, or humanitarian. But he did have galactic vision, and he was a great technologist. We need to learn from that. He was a genius of design, a charismatic showman, and a peerless marketer. He cultivated a penetrating and discerning eye for consumer preference and taste. He is one of the greatest visionaries in history. And that is so unbelievably unlikely. He was ousted from Apple in 1985, cast out from the company he had co-founded, only to return 11 years later "a very different person" as he would later say. But it was more than an unlikely comeback. His trajectory from that point was beyond imagination. In his second act, he would launch the iMac, the iPod, iTunes, the iPhone, and the iPad. He would literally change the world.

When Jobs was young, he was an enfant terrible—a loner, disruptive, and curious. After high school he went to college for six months and then dropped out. He became a smelly hippie and, by his own admission, had no idea what he wanted to do with his life. But he loved technology, so he wandered back home, and you know the rest of the story.

Jobs and his partner, Steve Wozniak, started Apple in the garage at the home of Jobs's parents. It was here that his unencumbered personality would find meaningful expression. Out of his disdain for convention; out of his prickly, brash, narcissistic demeanor; out of his vision, high drive, and confidence; out of his aesthetic instincts and deep emotional need to create something of elegant form and hyperfunction came an unprecedented string of exquisitely designed products and platforms.

Jobs had made mistakes in the past. He had crashed and burned. But he became more competent. He learned, changed, and exercised better judgment. When he did come back, he did so with astonishing vision. His competence went to a whole new level. Out of his failures, he refined his taste and elevated his unreasonable expectations. He developed an astonishing empathy for and connection with the consumer. "A lot of times," he said, "people don't know what they want until you show it to them."[6] He proved true his theory that simple can be harder than complex.

Jobs did not practice conventional corporate leadership. He was its implacable foe. Most organizations in the world foster incremental growth through incremental improvement. Most corporate leaders compete as a direct response to their competitors. They benchmark the herd. They look for best practices and, in the context of that arena, figure out what to do next. They lead in response to the measures and countermeasures of others. How much time do you think Jobs spent looking for best practices among his competitors?

Did he come up with all the ideas? Of course not. And that is part of the point. He cultivated a culture of independent thought and action in others because he had the seeds to plant it. We may not all possess the same galactic vision, but we can certainly challenge ourselves to push the borders of the vision we have today.

Vision and Creativity

What does vision have to do with creativity? Let me answer the question with a question: What drives creativity? Ideas. What drives ideas? Questions. If you trace the origin of creativity, you eventually find your way to a question. It was a question that led to the idea that led to the solution. But we are still not done with the causal chain. There are two more questions to ask: Who asked the question? That takes you to a real person. And, finally, why did that individual ask the question? There are various answers to the last *why* question: people ask questions for all sorts of reasons—need, interest, curiosity, exploration, fun, passion, pain, service, love, ambition, and competitiveness, to name a few.

Regardless of the particular motive, it all starts with a person who is willing to both ask a question and search for an answer. Many people are creative. I do not question that. But as important as creative drive is to creative genius, the quality of independent vision is just as important. It may be even *more* important. The vision to ask and pursue may be the single most important factor.

Steve Jobs observed, "Creativity is just connecting things. When you ask creative people how they did something, they feel a little guilty because they didn't really *do* it, they just *saw* something. It seemed obvious to them after a while. That's because they were able to connect experiences they've had and synthesize new things."[7] When I think about that statement, I ask why more people don't try to make new connections. Why don't more people have a sense of independent exploration?

Each year the MacArthur "Genius Grant" Fellowships are awarded annually to "talented individuals who have shown extraordinary originality and dedication in their creative pursuits and a marked capacity for self-direction."[8] That is the official statement from the McArthur Foundation. What it clarifies is the intimate relationship between vision and originality.

The implications are very important. We should cultivate independence before we cultivate creativity because the one is an enabling condition of the other. Independence spawns vision, creative thought, and action. In other words, people are independent before they are creative, not the other way around.

There is perhaps no more common pattern among creative geniuses. In fact, I suggest that you go to the MacArthur Foundation website and read profiles of the "Genius Grant" recipients because they are nothing alike except in their independent and visionary natures. Beyond the usual suspects of scientists and academics, the latest crop of fellows includes a playwright-composer, a sociologist, a tap dancer, a historian, a photographer, a painter, a community leader, a puppetry artist, and an education entrepreneur. As you watch these people interviewed, the common quality of vision is extraordinary.

One of the 2011 recipients, Peter Hessler, a long-form journalist, went to China for 10 years, mastered the language, and produced uncommonly rich accounts of a rapidly changing society.[9] Hessler has since moved with his family to Cairo, where he is learning Arabic and covering the Middle East for *The New Yorker*. His independent vision precedes his creativity. What if Hessler were highly risk- and loss-averse or spent a lot of time watching TV? He never would have left the country.

Author Denise Shekerjian discovered that "the creative person is one who can look at the same thing as everybody else but see something different. A creative act takes unremarkable parts to create an unforgettable whole."[10] In other words, creative people can see what others can't see. They have vision.

How else could Hessler produce rich narratives of China's rapidly urbanizing landscape? Certainly, there are hundreds of other journalists in China who see the same things. They see the same things, but Hessler sees more. He digs deeper. His powers of observation and interpretation are more highly developed. Why? Because he was more self-directed to immerse himself in the language and culture. He is more independent and therefore more creative and visionary.

Another MacArthur Fellow, Roland G. Fryer Jr., an African-American economist at Harvard who is striving to address racial inequality in the United States, flatly states, "I will not my let own personal views stand in the way of helping children."[11] That is a bold declaration of independence.

Simplify Your Vision

Can you think of a great vision that is complicated or confusing? We have torrents of data that tell us we are not very good at formulating and communicating vision. A number of studies show that approximately 80 percent of employees cannot accurately recite their organization's vision. Instead of vision we often apologize to organizations with sterile bromides, complex plans, shadowy ideas, or fuzzy aspirations. Our feckless efforts to give people a clear vision return skepticism and jaded complacency. Why does this happen over and over?

One reason is because you have to *earn* clarity. You have to work for it. Author and business executive Robert C. Townsend wrote, "Man is a complicating animal. He only simplifies under pressure."[12] It is the clarity of a vision that makes it powerful, that allows you to motivate people to eagle standards.

My grandfather's vision was simple: to overcome the adversity in his life and become a faithful husband, father, honest man, and contributing citizen. That vision draws its power out of its simplicity. A good vision is a masterpiece of compression. The clarity that arises from the compression stirs people and taps

Figure 8.1 The Role of Vision

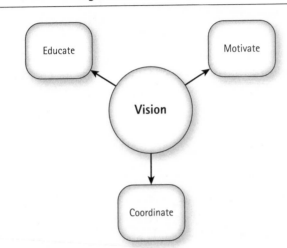

deep-seated emotions. Without that clarity, people improvise and work at cross purposes.

Operationally, a vision has three functions. First is the cognitive function to *educate*. Second is the emotional function to *motivate*. Third is the organizational function to *coordinate* (see figure 8.1). When we hit all three, a vision becomes the ultimate economy of scale and reduces the unit costs of making decisions by eliminating the ambiguity that might otherwise necessitate thousands of conversations. An effective vision provides for the mass production of answers and the creation of more-efficient and -effective coordinated action. Organizational metabolism, engagement, and productivity all rise together.

The two biggest threats to a strategic vision are that it will be changed or lost. Think about the predators that might bring a vision to its knees—interpretive filters, cultural bias, competing assumptions, informal networks, communication handoffs, and, not least, the editorial filter of the chain of command.

How's that for a gauntlet? There is one more barrier: the insecurity of the leader.

Insecure leaders are scared of simplicity, so they overcomplicate things to appear sophisticated. Here is the principle and the imperative, and my advice is the same whether you are a start-up or a Fortune 500 corporation:

- First, assume illiteracy.

- Second, assume oral tradition.

Communicate on the belief that no one can read and that the only way people can handle and pass on a vision is by talking about it. There is no pen, no paper, no Internet, no blog, no social network, no mediated discussion, no video, no podcast. There is nothing but a person's ability to carry the message in his or her head and communicate it to another human being face-to-face.

If you operate on these two assumptions, there's a good chance that the message will remain unmolested and able to withstand the damage-in-handling it will have to endure as it moves throughout the organization. If a vision is clear, it does not require PowerPoint, talking points, and a big marketing campaign. Put all of that gear down and pretend I can't read. Give it to me straight. And if you can't do that, the vision is not ready. Put it back in the oven. What organizational theorist Kenichi Ohmae said of strategy applies equally to vision: "Inability to articulate a strategy in a single, incisive, natural-sounding sentence is a sure sign that there is something wrong in the strategy itself."[13]

Communicate Your Vision

Let's remember that leadership is influence. Formulating a vision with others is a form of influence, but communicating that vision will be an even stronger form of influence. "Churchill mobilized the English language and sent it into battle," declared Edward R.

Murrow in a 1954 CBS broadcast.[14] Granted, few leaders will ever wield a literary sword like Churchill, but that is not the point. If you don't communicate well—if you can't get your point across in a clear, concise, and organized way—you have no choice but to spray and pray.

I am not suggesting that we can all become great communicators, but we can become good ones. Consider writing specifically. The American critic Ambrose Bierce explained,

> There is a good deal of popular ignorance about writing; it is commonly thought that good writing comes of a natural gift and that without the gift the trick cannot be learned. That is true of great writing, but not of good. Anyone of good natural intelligence and a fair education can be taught to write well, as well as he can be taught to draw well, or play billiards well, or shoot a rifle well, and so forth; to do any of these things greatly is another matter. If one cannot do great work, it is worthwhile to do good work and think it great.[15]

Forget about the finer points of style. That comes later. Let's just think about what it takes to do good work.

The American style of communicating, if there is one, is "clear, straight and plainspoken," wrote University of Chicago English professor Joseph M. Williams.[16] It sounds effortless to communicate in that way. Lucid communication is easy on the eyes and ears. In fact, the ease of consuming a clear message suggests the same ease of producing it. But, of course, that isn't true. An effective vision conceals its own labor.

In our modern society, things are working strongly against us. For example, we like to chunk our communications. Think about the sound bite or the 140-character tweet. Think about how texting has become its own shorn language. When my daughter texts, she uses incomplete sentences, as well as abbreviations like

TMI (too much information) and emoticons to convey thoughts and feelings. This isn't all bad, but it doesn't necessarily help you communicate well.

Further, the mass media sedates us. We become passive consumers of superficial content. With the average American watching five hours of television per day, most of us are far too busy to learn to communicate effectively.[17]

Not least, our public school system is engaged in a long-term retreat from English composition. The standard curriculum requires less writing than it used to. And even when students are assigned to write papers, teachers seldom read them, much less return them with heavy marginal notes. My middle-school-age children's papers are graded by a computer. They come home with high scores for clotted prose and low scores for clean prose. Can we be serious? Can a computer algorithm replace Mr. Westergard (my high-school English teacher) and his mentoring hand?

Communicating well is a discipline and an art. You have to practice. As novelist, journalist, and critic George Orwell explained, "Modern English, especially written English, is full of bad habits which spread by imitation and which can be avoided if one is willing to take the necessary trouble."[18] Learning to communicate well is like gaining control of a spirited horse. If you can harness its power, it will do great things for you. Eventually, it will turn on your gentle command, gallop on your signal, and jump when you say to. But don't expect to find a docile creature if you never spend time training it. That spirited horse will buck you off and run away.

Get a Vision of Your Life

Here is what I have to say about having a vision for your life: *get one*. You may have specific goals and aspirations, but I suggest that you devise a vision statement for your life that has nothing to do with title, position, or authority. Create an *I want to be remembered for...* statement, which will naturally turn you back to character, competence, and contribution.

Most people live far beneath their privileges because they lack vision or are tempted to aim low and be content when they achieve their aims. A vision should never include anything that promises to be easy, fast, or free. Nor should it be about seeing your name on a building, in lights, or behind glass. Those kinds of visions are shrines of self-worship.

Deep in our hearts we know we have a stewardship to leave things better than we found them. If we live our lives in the service of ourselves, our legacies will haunt us. But if we can learn from the past and from our own experience, we become better and more powerful leaders. As architect Daniel Burnham said, "Aim high in hope."[19]

VISION: SUMMARY POINTS

We all need vision to catalyze and sustain our efforts.

Dreams are things we want; visions are things we are willing to work for. Ask yourself if you are willing to work to achieve your vision.

When adversity strikes, tighten your grip on your vision. It will help you survive when thriving is not an option and you have to wait for a brighter day.

Reach back to your intergenerational identity as a source of vision in your own life. It will give you strength to overcome adversity.

Dare to break from convention and create your own galactic vision.

Your independent vision will precede your creativity.

Simplify and compress your vision until it has clarity.

Harness the power of language to create and communicate a powerful vision.

Get a vision of your life and leave a lasting legacy, rather than be haunted by the regret that you were not the leader you could have been.

Conclusion

It is not our part to master all the tides of the world,
but to do what is in us for the succour of those years wherein
we are set, uprooting the evil in the fields that we know,
so that those who live after may have clean earth to till.
What weather they shall have is not ours to rule.

J. R. R. Tolkien (1892–1973)
British writer, poet, philologist, and university professor
The Return of the King (1955)

TITLE, POSITION, AND AUTHORITY ARE NOT ONLY ACCESSO-
ries; they are beguiling ones. In the long run, they don't pay.
In and of themselves, they are meaningless objects of worship.
Writer David Foster Wallace described it thus:

> In the day-to-day trenches of adult life, there is actually
> no such thing as atheism. There is no such thing as not
> worshipping. Everybody worships. The only choice we get
> is what to worship....If you worship money and things, if
> they are where you tap real meaning in life, then you will
> never have enough, never feel you have enough. It's the
> truth. Worship your body and beauty and sexual allure
> and you will always feel ugly. And when time and age start
> showing, you will die a million deaths before they finally
> grieve you. On one level, we all know this stuff already.
> It's been codified as myths, proverbs, clichés, epigrams,
> parables; the skeleton of every great story. The whole trick
> is keeping the truth up-front in daily consciousness.

Worship power, you will end up feeling weak and afraid, and you will need ever more power over others to numb you to your own fear. Worship your intellect, being seen as smart, you will end up feeling stupid, a fraud, always on the verge of being found out.[1]

I hope we've settled any lingering misunderstanding that title, position, and authority can substitute for leadership. They cannot. More importantly, I hope a desire has welled up within you for something better, something more fulfilling, more lasting, and more real. If you simply look around, you will notice that chasing after these idols in the pursuit of your own success will leave you desolate. The trappings of power and praise are seductive, to the point that obtaining them has become a monstrous addiction. Abigail Adams wisely warned her husband, John Adams, "All men would be tyrants if they could."[2] Our society glorifies title, position, and authority and always has, even though we know the story ends badly for those who are so intoxicated. It's better to learn that lesson through observation than participation.

Remember novelist Leo Tolstoy's assessment of Napoleon: "And the genius Napoleon was defeated and taken to the island of St. Helena, having suddenly been discovered to be an outlaw. Whereupon the exile, parted from his dear ones and his beloved France, died a slow death on a rock, and bequeathed his great deeds to posterity. As for Europe, a reaction occurred there, and all the princes began to treat their peoples badly once again."[3]

In his brilliant and sardonic way, Tolstoy shows us this common human instinct. Most rulers in their hour or two on stage rearrange the furniture and then sleep with their fathers. But then somebody else comes along and moves the furniture again, rendering their exploits meaningless. History's long, nihilistic account of untrammeled greed, unbridled ambition, and unspectacular motive begs the question: *What is leadership?* It convicts the idea that it has anything to do with title, position, or authority. Across the sweep of history we must ask: *Who is truly a leader and who is a slave to small plans?*

The biblical account records that Jesus, apparently out of earshot of the thronging multitudes, gathered his disciples around him and, in a moment of profound private tutoring, compressed the concept of leadership to its elemental principle. He laid down the great and terrible truth: "But Jesus called them unto him, and said, Ye know that the princes of the Gentiles exercise dominion over them, and they that are great exercise authority upon them. But it shall not be so among you: but whosoever will be great among you, let him be your minister."[4]

He was saying that all of your life you have observed the common instinct—this pattern of rearranging the furniture and gratifying self. The Romans do it. The Hebrews do it. Then came the penetrating injunction: "But it shall not be so among you." Why? Because you are called to a greater work. You are called to lead. You are called to contribute rather than consume, bless rather than impress. How? Through inspired influence based on character and competence. With astounding clarity the Nazarene carpenter cut to the quick, and all of our metaphysical musings on the subject of leadership since have added nothing to this simple, unassailable truth.

The beauty of this discourse on leadership gives us a frame of reference—a sort of reflecting pool in which to see ourselves. It prompts us to ask honest questions about the nature of our intent and the manner of our influence. On the one hand, it is withering. There are times we would rather not look. But it is also hopeful because we know that leadership is within reach. The requirements are character and competence. There are no other barriers to entry.

A second carpenter taught me the lesson again. In my senior year of high school, I took a wood shop class from Ken Spencer. For my final project, I wanted to build a china cabinet for my mother for Christmas. After several weeks of plodding, I realized that I had been overzealous. I had neither the skills nor the time to finish the project. As Christmas drew near, I found myself falling behind and becoming discouraged. I would have nothing to give my mother.

With the holiday just days away, I walked into the shop on a Monday morning and, to my astonishment, there stood a completed china cabinet. It looked familiar and yet reflected expert craftsmanship. Mr. Spencer, who I always assumed was a rather stern, humorless man, said nothing. He offered a smile and then began his rounds, moving from student to student in his quiet, unassuming way. I was speechless. Why would my teacher do such a thing? He had obviously come in on the weekend to finish my project. As an insecure, struggling 17-year-old, I was shaken to the core by his gesture of kindness. I have never recovered and hope I never will.

The impact of that act has not diminished with time. To this day the china cabinet sits in my mother's kitchen as an enduring symbol of true leadership.

May we find joy in knowing that leadership can be found, and indeed is mostly found, in small and simple and unspectacular acts that influence others to do better and be better. Becoming a leader is a choice we get to make this very day and every day hereafter.[5]

This is the epic story of leadership.

Notes

Introduction

1. Spencer W. Kimball, "Jesus: The Perfect Leader," *Ensign*, August 1979.

2. C. S. Lewis, "Learning in War-Time," in *The Weight of Glory and Other Addresses* (Orlando, FL: Macmillan, 1980), 28.

3. Thomas Mann, *The Magic Mountain* (New York: Alfred P. Knopf, 1995), 181. First published 1924.

4. Albert Bandura, *Social Learning Theory* (New York: General Learning Press, 1971), 22.

5. Rik Kirkland, "How Dow Reinvented Itself," May 2016, McKinsey & Company, http://www.mckinsey.com/global-themes/leadership/how-dow-reinvented-itself.

6. Warren G. Bennis and Burt Nanus. *Leaders: Strategies for Taking Charge* (New York: Harper Business, 1997), 207.

7. William Wordsworth, "Character of the Happy Warrior," Poetry Foundation, April 25, 2016, http://www.poetryfoundation.org/poems-and-poets/poems/detail/45512.

8. Thomas Macaulay to a constituent, August 1832, accessed April 25, 2016, http://www.columbia.edu/itc/mealac/pritchett/00generallinks/macaulay/1832_1834_biog.html.

9. Daniel Kahneman, *Thinking, Fast and Slow* (New York: Farrar, Straus and Giroux, 2011), 35.

10. Rational-choice theorists would argue that people are actuated only by self-interest, especially economic self-interest. See, for instance, Amartya K. Sen, "Rational Fools: A Critique of the Behavioral Foundations of Economic Theory," *Philosophy & Public Affairs* 6, no. 4 (1977): 317–44. See also Jon Elster's "Introduction to Rational Choice," in *Rational Choice*, ed. Jon Elster (Oxford: Blackwell, 1986). Theoretically, the actor orders alternatives based on a subjective evaluation of consequences and then chooses the best one to accomplish a chosen end. The problem is that economic theory tells us nothing about what our aims ought to be. Economic theory has no explanatory power concerning moral imperatives. That's where morality comes in.

11. Barbara W. Tuchman, *A Distant Mirror: The Calamitous 14th* Century (New York: Alfred A. Knopf, 1978), 15.

12. Theodore Roosevelt, "Citizenship in a Republic" (speech, Sorbonne, Paris, France, April 23, 1910).

13. Simon Reynolds, ed., *Thoughts of Chairman Buffett: Thirty Years of Unconventional Wisdom from the Sage of Omaha* (New York: Harper Business, 2011), 64.

14. Thomas Paine, "The American Crisis," December 23, 1776, http://www.ushistory.org/paine/crisis/c-01.htm.

CHAPTER 1

The First Cornerstone of Character: Integrity

1. See "Corruption Perceptions Index 2015," Transparency International, accessed April 21, 2016, https://www.transparency.org.

2. Aristotle, *Politics,* Book 3, 1286a, accessed April 21, 2016, http://www.perseus.tufts.edu/hopper/text?doc=Perseus%3Atext%3A1999.01.0058%3Abook%3D3%3Asection%3D1286a.

3. Edelman Trust Barometer Executive Summary 2015, accessed April 21, 2016, http://www.edelman.com/insights/intellectual-property/2015-edelman-trust-barometer/trust-and-innovation-edelman-trust-barometer/executive-summary.

4. John Darwin, *After Tamerlane: The Global History of Empire Since 1405* (New York: Bloomsbury Press), 2008; see chapter 1 for context.

5. Charles Taylor gives a fascinating explanation of how we got to this point in his *A Secular Age* (Cambridge, MA: Harvard University Press, 2007). See chapter 13 in particular, which is ironically titled "The Age of Authenticity."

6. Gertrude Himmelfarb, *On Looking into the Abyss: Untimely Thoughts on Culture and Society* (New York: Vintage, 1995), 83.

7. Alexis de Tocqueville, *Democracy in America* (Anchor Press/Doubleday, 1969), 28. First published 1835.

8. Charles Dickens, *Hard Times* (Hertfordshire: Wordsworth Editions, 1995), 49. First published 1854.

9. Paul Johnson, "Militant Atheism and God," *Forbes,* September 21, 2007, http://www.forbes.com/forbes/2007/1008/027.html.

10. James. Q. Wilson, *The Moral Sense* (New York: Free Press, 1997), xi.

11. See the classic article by Albert Z. Carr, "Is Business Bluffing Ethical?" *Harvard Business Review,* January 1968, https://hbr.org/1968/01/is-business-bluffing-ethical.

28. Michael Lewis, *Liar's Poker* (New York: W.W. Norton, 2010), 87.

29. Peggy Noonan, "Hear, Hear," *Wall Street Journal*, September 29, 2007, http://www.wsj.com/articles/SB119101674787543050.

30. Elie Wiesel, *Night* (New York: Hill and Wang, 2006), 118.

31. Henry Mayer, *All on Fire: William Lloyd Garrison and the Abolition of Slavery* (New York: W. W. Norton, 2008), 631.

32. Press interview with Vince Lombardi, ca. 1958, recounted in Brian Tracy, "Brilliant on the Basics," Success.com, April 24, 2011, http://www.success.com/article/brilliant-on-the-basics.

33. Robert Louis Stevenson, *Memories and Portraits* (London: Chatto & Windus, 1887), from chapter 3, "Old Morality." The oft-cited quotation is a paraphrase of Stevenson's actual wording: "Books were the proper remedy: books of vivid human import, forcing upon their minds the issues, pleasures, busyness, importance and immediacy of that life in which they stand; books of smiling or heroic temper, to excite or to console; books of a large design, shadowing the complexity of *that game of consequences to which we all sit down,* the hanger-back not least." (italics added)

34. Thomas Hardy, *Far from the Madding Crowd* (New York: Penguin, 2003), 3. First published 1874.

35. Lawrence A. Cunningham, ed., *The Essays of Warren Buffett: Lessons for Corporate America* (Durham: Carolina Academic Press, 2015), 78.

36. Bob Moritz, "The U.S. Chairman of PwC on Keeping Millennials Engaged," *Harvard Business Review,* November 2014, 44, https://hbr.org/2014/11/the-us-chairman-of-pwc-on-keeping-millennials-engaged.

37. Company overview, Google, accessed April 27, 2016, https://www.google.com/about/company; and Transparency: Standards of business conduct, https://www.google.com/publicpolicy/transparency.html.

38. See Russell Hardin, "The Street-Level Epistemology of Trust," *Politics & Society* 21 (December 1993), 505–29.

39. Ralph Waldo Emerson, *The Conduct of Life* (Delaware: CreateSpace, 2016), 110. First published 1860.

CHAPTER 2

The Second Cornerstone of Character: Humility

Benjamin Franklin, *The Autobiography of Benjamin Franklin* (Mineola, New York: Dover Publications, 1996), 42. First published 1791.

12. Jon Meacham, *American Gospel: God, the Founding Fathers, an Making of a Nation* (New York: Random House, 2007), 405.

13. Don Meinert, "Creating an Ethical Workplace," *HR Magazir* no. 4 (April 2014), www.shrm.org/publications/hrmagazine/ed content/2014/0414/pages/0414-ethical-workplace-culture.aspx

14. Victor Hugo, *Les Miserables* (New York: Little, Brown & Cor 1887), 136.

15. Sir Walter Scott, *The Journal of Sir Walter Scott, 1825–183 the Original Manuscript at Abbotsford,* vol. I (May 6–7, 1831) Douglas, ed. (Edinburgh: David Douglas, 1891), 819.

16. Albert Schweitzer, *Out of My Life and Thought: An Autobi* (Johns Hopkins University Press, 2009), 154.

17. Would you cheat in an exam if you knew you wouldn't get cau Student Room, accessed April 21, 2016, http://www.thestud .co.uk/showthread.php?t=3650617.

18. Lou Gerstner, former CEO of IBM, said, "I manage by prin procedure." Louis V. Gerstner Jr., *Who Said Elephants Cai* (New York: Harper Business, 2002), 24.

19. Harvey C. Mansfield, "Have It Your Way," *Wall Street Journe* ber 16, 2006, http://www.wsj.com/articles/SB1163647096

20. Peggy Noonan, "Ronald Reagan," in *Character Above All* au series, vol. 6 (Simon & Schuster Audio, 1996).

21. Rik Kirkland, "Leading in the 21st Century: An Interview Vasella," September 2012, McKinsey & Company, http://ww .com/global-themes/leadership/an-interview-with-danie

22. John Calvin, *Institutes,* book II, chapter 2, no. 13 (1536).

23. Alexander Solzhenitsyn, "A World Split Apart" (spee University, Cambridge, MA, June 8, 1978).

24. Allan Bloom, *The Closing of the American Mind: How Hig Has Failed Democracy and Impoverished the Souls of To* (New York: Simon & Schuster, 2010), 201. Professor F on this point, but he does not admit that moral valu universal truths.

25. Horace Greeley, *The Autobiography of Horace Greeley: C of a Busy Life: to Which are Added Miscellaneous Ess* (New York: E. B. Treat, 1872), 143.

26. See Gordon Marino, "The Latest Industry to Flound *Wall Street Journal,* July 30, 2002, A14.

27. Wilson, *Moral Sense,* 226.

2. Edward Hess, *Learn or Die: Using Science to Build a Leading-Edge Learning Organization* (New York: Columbia University Press, 2015); see chapter 9.

3. Bill George, *Discover Your True North* (San Francisco: Jossey-Bass, 2015), 133.

4. Warren Berger, *A More Beautiful Question: The Power of Inquiry to Spark Breakthrough Ideas* (New York: Bloomsbury Press, 2014), 6.

5. Warren Bennis, *On Becoming a Leader* (New York: Basic Books, 2009), 2.

6. Proverbs 15:31–32 (Authorized [King James] Version).

7. Adam Bryant, "Narinder Singh of Topcoder: Is It the Cards, or How You Play Them?" *New York Times,* August 16, 2014, http://www .nytimes.com/2014/08/17/business/corner-office-narinder-singh-of -topcoder-is-it-the-cards-or-how-you-play-them.html?_r=0.

8. Walter Roy Harding, *The Thoreau Centennial: Papers Marking the Observance of the 100th Anniversary of the Death of Henry David Thoreau* (New York: State University of New York Press, 1964), 93.

9. Alison Beard, "Life's Work: An Interview with Salman Rushdie," *Harvard Business Review,* September 2015, 128, https://hbr .org/2015/09/lifes-work-salman-rushdie.

10. Rudyard Kipling, "Recessional," 1897, http://www.kiplingsociety.co.uk /rg_recess1.htm.

11. Chris Argyris, "Teaching Smart People How to Learn," *Harvard Business Review,* May-June 1991, https://hbr.org/1991/05/teaching-smart -people-how-to-learn.

12. F. Enzio Busche, "Unleashing the Dormant Spirit" (speech, Brigham Young University, May 14, 1996), http://kevinhinckley.com/userfiles /files/busche_fenzio_1996_05.pdf.

13. Richard Florida, *The Rise of the Creative Class* (New York: Basic Books), 2002, 14.

14. Kim Girard, "Recovering from the Need to Achieve," *HBS Working Knowledge,* June 27, 2011, http://hbswk.hbs.edu/item/recovering -from-the-need-to-achieve.

15. David Starr Jordan, *The Strength of Being Morally Clean: A Study of the Quest for Unearned Happiness* (Boston: H.M. Caldwell & Co., 1900), 43.

16. Herbert A. Simon, *Administrative Behavior* (New York: Free Press, 1997), 217.

17. John Huey, Geoffrey Colvin, Herb Kelleher, and Jack Welch, "The Jack and Herb Show," *Fortune,* January 11, 1999, http://archive.fortune

.com/magazines/fortune/fortune_archive/1999/01/11/253802/index
.htm.

CHAPTER 3

The Third Cornerstone of Character: Accountability

1. James Thomas Flexner, *Washington: The Indispensable Man* (New York: Signet Books), 1984, 35.

2. Sophocles, *The Seven Plays in English Verse,* "Antigone" (Jersey City: Start, 2015). First published ca. 441 BCE.

3. Jeffrey Pfeffer, "Petraeus and the Rise of Narcissistic Leaders," *Harvard Business Review,* November 12, 2012, https://hbr.org/2012/11 /petraeus-and-the-rise-of-narci.

4. Robert B. Cialdini, *Influence: The Psychology of Persuasion* (New York: Harper Business, 2006), 93.

5. Mohandas K. Gandhi, *All Men Are Brothers,* Krishna Kripalani, ed. (London: A & C Black, 2005), 106.

6. Will Durant and Ariel Durant, *The Lessons of History* (New York: Simon and Schuster, 1968), 35.

7. William McGurn, "Sex, Lies and Gmail," *Wall Street Journal,* November 12, 2012, http://www.wsj.com/articles/SB1000142412788732389 4704578115171159589036.

8. Ibid.

9. Daniel Gross, "The New Rules of the Game for CEOs," *Daily Beast,* November 11, 2012, http://www.thedailybeast.com/articles /2012/11/11/the-new-rules-of-the-game-for-ceos.html.

10. Elijah Adlow, *Napoleon in Italy: 1796–1797* (London: Pickle Partners, 1948), 189.

CHAPTER 4

The Fourth Cornerstone of Character: Courage

1. US Marine Corps, The Basic School, Marine Corps Training Command, Basic Officer Course, accessed April 23, 2016, http://www.trngcmd .marines.mil/Portals/207/Docs/TBS/B130736%20Ethics%20I.pdf.

2. Hugh Nibley, "Leaders and Managers," BYU Speeches, August 19, 1983, https://speeches.byu.edu/talks/hugh-nibley_leaders-managers.

3. Abraham Lincoln, "Lincoln's Farewell Address in Springfield, Illinois," 1861, accessed April 23, 2016, http://quod.lib.umich.edu/l/lincoln /lincoln4/1:306.1?rgn=div2;view=fulltext.

4. Carol Dweck, "Student Motivation: What Works, What Doesn't," *Education Week,* August 30, 2006, quoted at http://www.educationworld.com/a_issues/chat/chat010.shtml.

5. Admiral Hyman G. Rickover, "Thoughts on Man's Purpose in Life" (speech, New York City, May 12, 1982),

6. T. S. Eliot, preface to *Transit to Venue: Poems by Harry Crosby* (Boston: Black Sun Press, 1931), ix.

7. Jessica Mintz, "Gates Bids Farewell to Fulltime Work at Microsoft with Tears," ABC News, accessed April 23, 2016, http://abcnews.go.com/Business/story?id=5270034.

8. Adam Bryant, "Satya Nadella, Chief of Microsoft, in His New Role," *New York Times,* February 20, 2014, http://www.nytimes.com/2014/02/21/business/satya-nadella-chief-of-microsoft-on-his-new-role.html.

9. John Chambers, "John Chambers on Keeping Cisco on Top," August 23, 2012, http://www.bloomberg.com/news/articles/2012-08-23/john-chambers-on-keeping-cisco-on-top.

10. Emily Dickinson, "Tell all the truth but tell it slant," accessed April 23, 2016, http://www.poetryfoundation.org/poem/247292.

11. Ed Cray, *General of the Army: George C. Marshall, Solider and Statesman* (New York: Cooper Square Press, 2000), 88.

12. Harvey Schachter, "Subordinates Urged to Speak Up," *The Globe and Mail,* March 27, 2002, http://www.theglobeandmail.com/news/world/subordinates-urged-to-speak-up/article20436621.

13. Jeff Dyer, Hal Gregersen, and Nathan Furr, "Decoding Tesla's Secret Formula," *Forbes,* September 7, 2015, http://www.forbes.com/sites/innovatorsdna/2015/08/19/teslas-secret-formula.

14. "The Shackleton Expedition," The Mark of a Leader, accessed April 23, 2016, http://www.themarkofaleader.com/the-shackleton-expedition.

15. "Debt," Monticello.org, accessed April 28, 2016, https://www.monticello.org/site/research-and-collections/debt.

16. G. K. Chesterton, *All Things Considered* (Seattle: Amazon Digital Services, 2012), 63. First published 1908.

17. Jonathan Swift, *The Works of Jonathan Swift,* vol. 6 (New York: Derby & Jackson, 1859), 22.

18. Mark Twain, *Bite-Size Twain: Wit and Wisdom from the Literary Legend,* eds. John P. Holms and Karin Baji (New York: St. Martin's Press, 1998), 74.

19. Robert Browning, "Andrea del Sarto," 1855, http://www.poetryfoundation.org/poem/173001.

CHAPTER 5

The First Cornerstone of Competence: Learning

1. Edgar H. Schein makes a similar point. See his "How Can Organizations Learn Faster? The Challenge of Entering the Green Room," *Sloan Management Review,* January 15, 1993, http://sloanreview.mit.edu /article/how-can-organizations-learn-faster-the-challenge-of-entering -the-green-room.

2. Ken Bain, *What the Best College Teachers Do* (Cambridge, MA: Harvard University Press, 2004), 55.

3. Michael McKinney, "Lincoln's Lessons: Invest in Who You Are," February 13, 2009, http://www.leadershipnow.com/leadingblog/2009 /02/lincolns_lessons_invest_in_who.html.

4. "MIT Media Lab's Joi Ito on Digital Innovation and Disruption," BCG Perspectives, March 22, 2016, www.bcgperspectives.com/content /videos/technology-ito-joi-digital-innovation-disruption/?utm _source=201603TechDigital&utm_medium=Email&utm_campaign =otr.

5. Robert J. Grossman, "IBM's HR Takes a Risk," *HR Magazine,* April 1, 2007, https://www.shrm.org/publications/hrmagazine/editorialcontent /pages/0407grossman.aspx.

6. John Seely Brown and Paul Duguid, *The Social Life of Information* (Cambridge, MA: Harvard Business Review Press, 2002), 136.

7. Patricia Sellers, "Starbucks' Schultz: From Cocky to Vulnerable," *Fortune,* July 31, 2008, http://fortune.com/2008/07/31/starbucks -schultz-from-cocky-to-vulnerable.

8. Thomas A. Stewart, *Intellectual Capital: The New Wealth of Organization* (New York: Bantam Doubleday, 1999), xx.

9. Jacob Morgan. *The Future of Work: Attract New Talent, Build Better Leaders, and Create a Competitive Organization* (New York: Wiley, 2014), 32.

10. Charles Eliot, "The Durable Satisfactions of Life" (speech, Harvard University, October 3, 1905), printed in *McClure's Magazine,* vol. 26 (1906).

11. John Stuart Mill, *Utilitarianism,* chapter 2, "What Utilitarianism Is" (1863), accessed April 23, 2016, http://www.utilitarianism.com/mill2 .htm.

12. V. S. Naipaul, *A Writer's People: Ways of Looking and Feeling* (New York: Alfred A. Knopf, 2007), 17.

13. Peter Galison, Gerald James Holton, and Silvan S. Schweber, eds., *Einstein for the 21st Century: His Legacy in Science, Art, and Modern Culture* (Princeton: Princeton University Press, 2008), 222.

14. Anya Kamenetz, "Bill Gates on Education: 'We Can Make Massive Strides,'" *Fast Company,* April 15, 2013, http://www.fastcompany .com/3007841/tech-forecast/bill-gates-education-we-can-make -massive-strides.

15. Nick Collins, "Sir John Gurdon, Nobel Prize Winner, Was 'Too Stupid' for Science at School," *The Telegraph,* October 8, 2012, http:// www.telegraph.co.uk/news/science/science-news/9594351/Sir-John -Gurdon-Nobel-Prize-winner-was-too-stupid-for-science-at-school .html.

16. Winston Churchill, "The Bright Gleam of Victory" (speech, Mansion House, London, November 10, 1942), http://www.winstonchurchill .org/resources/speeches/1941-1945-war-leader/987-the-end-of-the -beginning.

17. K. Anders Ericsson, Michael J. Prietula, and Edward T. Cokely, "The Making of an Expert," *Harvard Business Review,* July-August 2007, https://hbr.org/2007/07/the-making-of-an-expert.

18. Geoff Colvin, *Talent Is Overrated: What Really Separates World-Class Performers from Everybody Else* (New York: Portfolio, 2010), 89.

19. Don Tapscott and Anthony D. Williams. *Wikinomics: How Mass Collaboration Changes Everything* (New York: Portfolio, 2008), 55.

CHAPTER 6

The Second Cornerstone of Competence: Change

1. Rob Norton, "The Thought Leader Interview: Sylvia Nasar," *Strategy+Business,* August 23, 2011, http://www.strategy-business .com/article/11311?gko=72d26.

2. Drucker Institute, "A Topic We Just Can't Seem to Abandon," January 4, 2012, http://www.druckerinstitute.com/2012/01/a-topic-we-just-cant -seem-to-abandon.

3. Martin E. P. Seligman, "Building Resilience," *Harvard Business Review,* April 2011, https://hbr.org/2011/04/building-resilience.

4. John R. Ehrenfeld, "The Roots of Sustainability," *MIT Sloan Management Review* 46, no. 2 (2005): 23–25, http://sloanreview.mit.edu /article/the-roots-of-sustainability.

CHAPTER 7

The Third Cornerstone of Competence: Judgment

1. Howard Gardner, *Five Minds for the Future* (Cambridge, MA: Harvard Business School Press, 2009); see chapter 3.

2. Noel Tichy and Warren Bennis, "Making Judgment Calls," *Harvard Business Review,* October 2007, https://hbr.org/2007/10/making -judgment-calls.

3. "Marc Andreessen on Big Breakthrough Ideas and Courageous Entrepreneurs" (Stanford Graduate School of Business video), accessed April 23, 2016, http://www.getlinkyoutube.com/watch?v=JYYsXzt1VDc.

4. Benjamin Graham, *The Intelligent Investor: The Definitive Book on Value Investing* (New York: Harper Business, 2005), 524.

5. David F. Gallagher and Brad Stone, "Jerry Yang, Yahoo Chief, Plans to Step Down," *New York Times,* November 17, 2008, http://bits .blogs.nytimes.com/2008/11/17/jerry-yang-yahoo-chief-plans-to-step -down.

6. "Warren Buffett on Charlie Rose: Notes," Seeking Alpha, July 24, 2006, http://seekingalpha.com/article/14114-warren-buffett-on-charlie -rose-notes.

7. Keith H. Hammonds, "Michael Porter's Big Ideas," *Fast Company,* February 28, 2001, http://www.fastcompany.com/42485/michael -porters-big-ideas.

8. Judges 9:4 (Authorized [King James] Version).

9. Antoine de Saint-Exupéry, *The Little Prince* (New York: Houghton, Mifflin, Harcourt, 2015), 22.

10. John W. Gardner, "Leadership: Attributes and Context," *NASSP Bulletin,* February 1989, http://bul.sagepub.com/content/73/514/58 .extract.

11. Niccolo Machiavelli, *The Prince* (New York: Signet Classics, 1999); see chapter 22. First published 1513.

12. D. Michael Abrashoff, *It's Your Ship: Management Techniques from the Best Damn Ship in the Navy* (New York: Grand Central, 2012), 4.

13. Lawrence A. Cunningham, ed., *The Essays of Warren Buffett: Lessons for Corporate America* (Durham: Carolina Academic Press, 2015), 294.

14. Edgar Schein, *Humble Inquiry: The Gentle Art of Asking Instead of Telling* (San Francisco: Berrett-Koehler, 2013), 5.

15. Karl E. Weick and Kathleen M. Sutcliffe, *Managing the Unexpected: Assuring High Performance in an Age of Complexity* (San Francisco: Jossey-Bass, 2001), 55.

CHAPTER **8**

The Fourth Cornerstone of Competence: Vision

1. I like Peter M. Senge's statement: "Truly creative people use the gap between vision and current reality to generate energy for change." *The Fifth Discipline: The Art & Practice of the Learning Organization* (New York: Doubleday, 1990), 153.

2. James Champy and Nitin Nohria, *The Arc of Ambition: Defining the Leadership Journey* (New York: Basic Books, 2001), 29.

3. Erich Fromm, *Man for Himself: An Inquiry into the Psychology of Ethics* (New York: Holt Paperbacks, 1990); see chapter 3.

4. Bruce Feiler, "The Stories That Bind Us," *New York Times,* March 15, 2013, http://www.nytimes.com/2013/03/17/fashion/the-family-stories-that-bind-us-this-life.html.

5. Steve Jobs, "You've Got to Find What You Love" (speech, Stanford University, June 12, 2005), http://news.stanford.edu/news/2005/june15/jobs-061505.html.

6. Andy Reinhardt, "Steve Jobs: 'There's Sanity Returning,'" *BusinessWeek,* May 25, 1998. http://www.businessweek.com/1998/21/b3579165.htm.

7. Gary Wolf, "Steve Jobs, "The Next Insanely Great Thing," *Wired,* February 1, 1996, http://www.wired.com/1996/02/jobs-2.

8. "About the MacArthur Fellows Program," MacArthur Foundation, accessed May 2, 2016, https://www.macfound.org/pages/about-macarthur-fellows-program.

9. MacArthur Fellows Program: Peter Hessler, MacArthur Foundation, September 20, 2011, https://www.macfound.org/fellows/8.

10. Denise Shekerjian, *Uncommon Genius: How Great Ideas Are Born* (New York: Penguin Books, 1990), 17.

11. MacArthur Fellows Program: Roland Fryer, MacArthur Foundation, September 20, 2011, https://www.macfound.org/fellows/3.

12. Robert C. Townsend, *Up the Organization: How to Stop the Corporation from Stifling People and Strangling Profit* (San Francisco: Jossey-Bass, 2007), 132.

13. Kenichi Ohmae, *The Mind of the Strategist: The Art of Japanese Business* (New York: McGraw-Hill, 1991), 253.

14. George R. Goethals, Georgia Jones Sorenson, and James MacGregor Burns, eds., *Encyclopedia of Leadership: A–E,* vol. 1 (Thousand Oaks, CA: Sage), 185.

15. Ambrose Bierce, *The Collected Works of Ambrose Bierce*, vol. 10 (New York: Neale, 1911), 75.

16. Joseph M. Williams, *Style: Toward Clarity and Grace* (Chicago: University of Chicago Press, 1995), 9.

17. David Hinckley, "Average American Watches 5 Hours of TV per Day, Report Shows," *New York Daily News,* March 5, 2014, http://www .nydailynews.com/life-style/average-american-watches-5-hours-tv -day-article-1.1711954.

18. George Orwell, "Politics and the English Language." First published in *Horizon* (London, April 1946), accessed April 23, 2016, http://www .orwell.ru/library/essays/politics/english/e_polit.

19. Charles Moore, *Daniel H. Burnham, Architect, Planner of Cities,* vol. 2 (Charleston: Nabu Press, 2010), 147. First published 1921.

Conclusion

1. David Foster Wallace, "What Is Water?" (speech, Kenyon College, Gambier, Ohio, 2005), accessed April 23, 2016, https://www.1843magazine .com/story/david-foster-wallace-in-his-own-words.

2. Abigail Adams to John Adams, March 31, 1776, accessed April 23, 2016, http://www.pbs.org/wgbh/amex/adams/filmmore/ps_ladies .html.

3. Leo Tolstoy, *War and Peace* (New York: Penguin Books, 2009), epilogue part 2. First published 1869.

4. Matthew 20:25–26 (Authorized [King James] Version).

5. Reinhold Niebuhr, *The Children of Light and the Children of Darkness: A Vindication of Democracy and a Critique of Its Traditional Defense* (New York: Charles Scribner Sons, 1944), 19.

Leading with Character and Competence Self-Assessment

IF YOUR TOLERANCE FOR CANDOR IS HIGH, YOU MAY BE interested in the Leading with Character and Competence Self-Assessment companion product referenced in the preface.

This 80-item online self-assessment instrument, which takes approximately 10 to 15 minutes to complete, is a powerful and psychometrically validated tool that addresses each of the cornerstones of character and competence. It is available at bkconnection.com/character+competence-sa.

The self-assessment will help you understand the degree to which you have developed and are currently applying the cornerstones of character and competence in your personal and professional lives.

The instrument is designed to take you to penetrating new levels of self-awareness in your leadership journey and motivate you to improve your performance through reflection, goal setting, commitment, and deliberate practice. Your graphical results will include interpretation and development tips.

You may print out your customized Leading with Character and Competence profile and retake the self-assessment up to four times within a 12-month period. Bulk-order discounts are available for organizations.

Acknowledgments

I THANK MY REVIEWERS—JAMES HOLT, JAN NICKERSON, Jeffrey Kulick, and Bryan Rodriguez—for testing my tolerance for candor, contributing penetrating insight, and helping me see my weaknesses more clearly. To Steve Piersanti, Jeevan Sivasubramaniam, Neal Maillet, and the entire team at Berrett-Koehler, I express my deep gratitude for taking on this project and engaging in a true partnership. I gratefully acknowledge the skill and judgment of Elizabeth von Radics for copyediting and Gary Palmatier for interior design and layout. On the home front, I thank my three sons (the experimental group) and my three daughters (the control group). Indeed the family is the ultimate leadership laboratory. Finally, to my wife, Tracey, my confidant, trusted adviser, and faithful companion, thank you for your love, wisdom, and guidance.

Index

The letter *f* following a page number denotes a figure.

About the Author

Timothy R. Clark is founder and CEO of LeaderFactor, a consulting and training firm that focuses on leadership development, change management, and strategic agility. He is also co-founder of BlueEQ, an emotional intelligence assessment and training firm.

Clark is regarded as a global authority on leadership, large-scale change, and strategic agility. He consults, trains, and coaches leadership teams around the world. Clark has written three previous books and more than 100 articles. A former two-time CEO and first-team academic all-American football player at Brigham Young University, Clark earned a doctorate from Oxford University in social sciences and politics. He and his wife, Tracey, are the parents of three sons and three daughters.

Berrett–Koehler
Publishers

Berrett-Koehler is an independent publisher dedicated to an ambitious mission: *connecting people and ideas to create a world that works for all.*

We believe that to truly create a better world, action is needed at all levels—individual, organizational, and societal. At the individual level, our publications help people align their lives with their values and with their aspirations for a better world. At the organizational level, our publications promote progressive leadership and management practices, socially responsible approaches to business, and humane and effective organizations. At the societal level, our publications advance social and economic justice, shared prosperity, sustainability, and new solutions to national and global issues.

A major theme of our publications is "Opening Up New Space." Berrett-Koehler titles challenge conventional thinking, introduce new ideas, and foster positive change. Their common quest is changing the underlying beliefs, mindsets, institutions, and structures that keep generating the same cycles of problems, no matter who our leaders are or what improvement programs we adopt.

We strive to practice what we preach—to operate our publishing company in line with the ideas in our books. At the core of our approach is stewardship, which we define as a deep sense of responsibility to administer the company for the benefit of all of our "stakeholder" groups: authors, customers, employees, investors, service providers, and the communities and environment around us.

We are grateful to the thousands of readers, authors, and other friends of the company who consider themselves to be part of the "BK Community." We hope that you, too, will join us in our mission.

A BK Business Book

This book is part of our BK Business series. BK Business titles pioneer new and progressive leadership and management practices in all types of public, private, and nonprofit organizations. They promote socially responsible approaches to business, innovative organizational change methods, and more humane and effective organizations.

Berrett–Koehler
Publishers

Connecting people and ideas
to create a world that works for all

Dear Reader,

Thank you for picking up this book and joining our worldwide community of Berrett-Koehler readers. We share ideas that bring positive change into people's lives, organizations, and society.

To welcome you, we'd like to offer you a free e-book. You can pick from among twelve of our bestselling books by entering the promotional code **BKP92E** here: http://www.bkconnection.com/welcome.

When you claim your free e-book, we'll also send you a copy of our e-newsletter, the *BK Communiqué*. Although you're free to unsubscribe, there are many benefits to sticking around. In every issue of our newsletter you'll find

- A free e-book
- Tips from famous authors
- Discounts on spotlight titles
- Hilarious insider publishing news
- A chance to win a prize for answering a riddle

Best of all, our readers tell us, "Your newsletter is the only one I actually read." So claim your gift today, and please stay in touch!

Sincerely,

Charlotte Ashlock
Steward of the BK Website

Questions? Comments? Contact me at bkcommunity@bkpub.com.

Certified
Corporation
bcorporation.net